D1253752

POCKET DICTIONARY OF COLLECTOR'S TERMS

POCKET DICTIONARY OF COLLECTOR'S TERMS

MICHAEL GOODWIN 1916-

Illustrations by C. Dampier Freeman

PHILOSOPHICAL LIBRARY

FOR ALISON

Published, 1967, by Philosophical Library, Inc.
15 East 40th Street, New York 16, N.Y.
All rights reserved
Printed and Bound in Great Britain by
Hazell Watson & Viney Limited
Aylesbury, Bucks

Contents

5

Contents

Introduction

This book is for the collector, for the man or woman who is attracted to objects which are beautiful or in some way curious and which have a history. Such objects are to be found up and down the country in auction rooms, in house sales, in antique shops, and even what are commonly named 'junk' shops. They are also, of course, to be found in the homes of one's friends and, more frequently than one would care to confess, one has lived for years with them around one without knowing or bothering to discover their true identity.

The purpose of the book is twofold: to aid the reader in his purchases and to add to his knowledge, and therefore appreciation, of the antique and of the skills of past craftsmen. What is not intended is to cater for the needs of the millionaire collector or even the spender of thousands of pounds on a single item. For them there is already a considerable literature, far more extensive than that currently available to the connoisseur in spirit with all too modest means.

If it should be said that many of the entries in this book are taken up with descriptions of collectors' items far beyond the purse of those for whom it is written, there is a reason for this. There is a tradition of craftsmanship; many relatively humble pieces owe their inspiration, as did their makers, to 'patrician' antecedents. History is not merely the record of kings, nor yet even of their achievements. The rare and, in a few instances, the singular have therefore been included deliberately to give perspective to the more familiar.

The divisions of the book are between furniture, glass, silver and other metals, china, carpets, and bijouterie—a convenient portmanteau term to include numerous small items such as fans, clocks, paperweights, etc. In addition there is a section on leading craftsmen and manufacturers. All are separately arranged in alphabetical order and, where necessary, cross-referenced. As its modest proportions would suggest, the book is not encyclopaedic in its comprehension of categories, terms or descriptions. One has to be arbitrary in a work of this nature. Numerous items have been omitted as warranting either too much or scarcely any description; others have simply had to give way to a prearranged order of priorities.

A knowledge of carpets constitutes, perhaps, a marginal need in the experience of many who will read this book, but they possess an exotic and exclusive interest in relation to many of the other categories and a little knowledge of them provides one with frequent opportunities for the irresistible game of private detection. For the rest the items have been chosen to comprise so far as is possible the reader's likely range of purchases and scope of interests.

Inevitably in a task of this kind one is obliged to lean— sometimes, albeit reluctantly, heavily—on the skilled researches and compilations of others. One merely attempts to spread one's obligations as thinly as possible. In the preparation of *The Country Life Pocket Dictionary of Collector's Terms* I am deeply conscious of the debt I owe to existing authorities and, in particular, to those listed in the bibliography on p. 316 by whose previous efforts in this field I have been largely borne along.

My unstinting gratitude is also due to my research assistant, Miss Eirene Skilbeck, whose industry and patient good humour have consistently smoothed the way for my own contribution.

1967   *Michael Goodwin*

PART ONE

Pottery and Porcelain

'A' Mark. Associated with Bow porcelain.

Acid Gilding. Process of etching patterns into china, usually in the form of a border, and covering with gold; first introduced by Mintons in 1863.

Acoustic Jars. Name given to pottery vessels found within the fabric of many medieval churches.

Adam and Eve. Popular subject on delftware 'chargers' (from 1635), slipware and stoneware groups.

'Admiral Lord Howe' Jug. Variety of Toby jug, the subject being a naval figure seated.

'A F' Mark. Associated with Bow porcelain.

Agate Ware. Salt-glazed stoneware or lead-glazed earthenware made in the likeness of agate and other stones by the juxtaposition of different coloured clays. Semi-precious stone effect imitated by Josiah Wedgwood.

Adam and Eve decoration

Agate Ware cat

9

Albany Slip. The diluted, creamy state of a fine, rich brown clay found on the banks of the River Hudson, near Albany, New York.

Albarello. Maiolica drug-pot introduced into Italy from Spain and later copied by English tin-glazed earthenware makers.

Albarello: maiolica drug-pot

Alcora Maiolica. Fine quality tin-glazed earthenware made in the early 18th century at Alcora in Valencia, Spain.

Amstel Porcelain. Hard-paste porcelain, with fine white body resembling Dresden, decorated with landscape and figure subjects, made near Amsterdam (1764–1810).

An Hua. 'Secret' decoration engraving or painting found on early Ming and 18th-century Chinese white porcelain, so faint as to be visible only when held to the light.

Anchor Marks. Associated with Chelsea, Bow, Derby, Davenport, Sceaux and Venice porcelain.

Angoulême Porcelain. Hard-paste porcelain made in Paris (1780–1829); notable for successful reproduction of under-glaze coloured ground used at Sèvres and the colours for on-glaze painting.

Ansbach Porcelain. Hard-paste porcelain manufactured in the 18th and 19th centuries at Ansbach, Bavaria. Borrowed many of its modelled figures from Meissen; its tablewares were influenced by Berlin and Nymphenburg.

Anchor marks. FIRST ROW. Four Chelsea, 1749–52; Red, 1752–6; Red, 1752–6; Gold, 1758–69. Two Bow: Blue and Red, 1760–76. SECOND ROW. Two Bow: Blue and Red, 1760–76. Chelsea–Derby: 1770. Two Derby: 1770–80; 1777. Two Davenport: 1793–1890. THIRD ROW. Four Sceaux: Blue, 1748; Blue, 1748; Blue, 1748; 1775. Three Venice: Red, 1765; Gold, 1700; Red, 1765–1811

'Apostle' Jug. Made by Charles Meigh, c. 1845. Bears relief figures of the Apostles under Gothic arcading.

'Apple-green'. Ground colour introduced at Sèvres in 1757 and used by Worcester from 1770.

Ansbach Porcelain

11

'A R' Mark. Found on Meissen porcelain made for King Frederick Augustus the Strong of Saxony.

Arcanist. From *arcanum* (L.) meaning a secret. Name given to one initiated into the secrets of pottery-making and, more especially, porcelain-making.

'A R' mark

Arcanum. The chemical composition and technique of porcelain-making.

Argil. Clay; usually with reference to potters' clay.

Argyle. Gravy container of silver, plate or pottery with outer lining or central container for hot water; c. 1770–1820.

Arita Porcelain. The first Japanese porcelain kilns were established at Arita. The two styles developed there, the Kakiemon and the 'Imari', were exported to Europe where they were widely copied.

Armorial China. Services of porcelain bearing coats of arms and crests, popular in the 18th century. Until the mid-18th century, made in China from references supplied (e.g. book-plates, engravings, etc.); later by the Worcester, Bristol, Wedgwood and Leeds factories.

Arras Porcelain. Soft-paste porcelain made in Pas-de-Calais from 1770–90. The period 1782–6 is notable for the production of wares said to rival those of Sèvres.

Arrow Mark. Associated with Worcester and Pinxton porcelain.

Ashet. Large meat plate (Scottish).

'Astbury'. Type ware. Classification of Staffordshire pottery produced c. 1730–40 in a combination of red and white clays under a transparent lead glaze; as distinct from 'Astbury-

'Astbury' figure

Bamboo ware bulb pot

Barber's Dish

Whieldon' ware in which the glaze is splashed or dabbed with metallic oxides.

'B' Mark. Associated with Bow, Bristol and Worcester porcelain.

Ball Clay. A clay from Devon and Dorset used in the manufacture of earthenware. Also called Blue Clay.

Ballot Box. Also known as SALT-KIT. Dome-topped jar, used for storing salt, with loop handle and circular aperture at side.

'Bamboo' Ware. Stoneware made by Josiah Wedgwood in imitation of bamboo.

Barber's Dish. Circular dish with cutaway portion to fit the neck.

Barberini Vase. See PORTLAND VASE. Sir William Hamilton purchased the Portland Vase from the Barberini family in 1770.

13

Basaltes: black stoneware jug. 'Battle for the Breeches'.
Beaker in porcelain

Barm Pot. Used for storing barm (froth of fermenting liquor) or yeast. See also BALLOT BOX.

Basaltes. Unglazed fine-grained black stoneware made by Wedgwood and others.

Bason. 17th- and 18th-century spelling for basin or large vessel.

Bassano Porcelain. 18th-century Italian soft-paste porcelain decorated in deep blue in the oriental manner similar to Doccia and Venice porcelain.

Bat. Slab of coarse clay used for building up the ware in the kiln or oven during firing.

Bat-printing. Method of transfer-printing on glazed pottery from engraved copper-plates and gelatine or linseed oil. Late 18th and early 19th century.

'Batavian Ware'. Named after Javanese port of export to Europe in the early 18th century. Chinese porcelain with brown-glazed ground and panels of *famille rose* decoration.

'Battle for the Breeches'. Theme depicting the fight for supremacy between husband and wife adopted as subject matter on 17th-century slipware and 19th-century spill vases.

Beaker. Handleless drinking vessel, usually of tapering cylindrical form.

Bear Jug.   Belleek dish with cover.   Bellarmine: ale-house bottle

Bear Jug. Jug shaped as bear hugging dog, made in stoneware in Staffordshire, Nottingham, Derby and Yorkshire. 18th and early 19th century.

Bell Ringers' Jug. Ale jugs for the bell ringers, retained either in the church tower or at the bell ringer's home.

Bellarmine. Also known as GREY BEARD or LONG BEARD because of a bearded mask opposite the handle. A stoneware ale-house bottle named after Cardinal Bellarmino (1542–1621). Associated with early witchcraft because examples have frequently been unearthed containing charms against evil spirits.

Belleek. A light, fragile felspathic porcelain with pearly glaze made from 1857 onwards by the factory of David McBirney & Co. at Belleek in Ireland. Made in America in the late 19th century; also in East Liverpool where it was called LOTUS WARE.

Belper Pottery. Made at Belper in Derbyshire from the mid-18th century.

Bennington. From the town of Bennington in Vermont; the name has been applied to American brown Rockingham wares.

Berlin Porcelain. Rival to Meissen; a hard-paste porcelain,

'BFB' mark   **Bin label for hock**

decorated in the classical manner; also service pieces finely painted with German garden and landscape scenes.

'B F B' Mark. Associated with Worcester porcelain of the period 1807–13, when the partnership was 'Barr, Flight & Barr'.

Bianco Sopra Bianco. Form of mid-18th-century white earthenware decoration on pale grey or blue ground used at the Lambeth, Bristol and Liverpool factories.

'Billy Waters'. 19th-century London character who became a popular pottery subject; a black fiddler with a wooden leg.

Bin Label. Late 17th century; pottery label to be hung beside wine bin.

Bird Call. Pottery whistle fashioned in the shape of a bird.

Bird Fountain. 18th- and 19th-century earthenware wall bracket with container for water.

Biscuit (Bisque). Fired porcelain or pottery before glazing or painting.

Biscuit figure (Sèvres Porcelain)

16

Black-glazed Pottery cat   **Blanc-de-Chine figure**

Black Egyptian Ware. See BASALTES.

Black-glazed Pottery. Red earthenware with lustrous black or brownish-black glaze, made in Burslem in the second half of the 18th century and in Shropshire.

Black-printing. The application of impressions to glazed vessels, whether the colour be black, red or gold.

Blanc-de-Chine. Porcelain made at Te-Hua in the Province of Fukien during the Ming dynasty, distinct for its wide variations of white.

Bleu-de-Ciel. With BLEU-DU-ROI, BLEU CELESTE and BLEU PERSAN, colours used in the decoration of Sèvres porcelain.

Blue Clay. See BALL CLAY.

Blue John. Also known as Derbyshire spar. Calcite, or native carbonate of lime, of a violet-blue colour much used for decorative purposes in the second half of the 18th and in the 19th century.

Blue or Lavender Glazes. Particularly fine porcelain with a high-temperature cobalt-blue glaze made during the Ming period.

'Blue-and-White' Chinese Porcelain. Traditional decoration with painting in cobalt blue under the glaze.

17

Blue-dash Chargers. Circular Delftware dishes with, in addition to figural or floral decorations, blue dashes at the edge. 17th and 18th century.

'Bocage'. The background to earthenware figures of the 18th and 19th century: foliage or tree compositions.

Blue-dash charger

Example of 'bocage'

'Boccaro' Ware. In fact, Yi-hsing unglazed red and brown Chinese stoneware teapots imported into Europe from the late 17th century.

Body. The essential pottery ware or stoneware; in the case of porcelain, paste (hard or soft).

Bologna. Factory established in Italy in the mid-19th century for the manufacture of majolica; notable for the reproduction of the old Luce della Robbia and Urbino ware.

Bone China. Standard English porcelain since the beginning of the 19th century; hard-paste mixed with bone-ash (which might constitute up to 40% of the whole).

Bordeaux. Factory for the manufacture of hard-paste porcelain, established c. 1784.

Boston Earthenware Manufacturing Co. Pottery operated by Frederick Mear (1822–76) from Burslem, which made brown-mottled yellow ware.

Botanical Flowers. Species of floral decoration originating

Bow candle-stick

Bristol cup and saucer

with Meissen, and thereafter much used by a number of leading English porcelain makers.

Bourg-la-Reine. See MENNECY PORCELAIN.

Bow. Porcelain from the factory at Stratford-le-Bow, London, founded c. 1745, and active for 20–30 years.

Bradwell Wood Pottery. Generally accepted to be the site of one of the Elers' (brothers) factory in the late 17th century; notable for the production of 'red china' teapots.

Brampton Stoneware. Brown stoneware made in the 18th and 19th centuries; examples from 1820–94 are distinguished for their internal green glaze.

Bratina. Form of loving-cup, native to Russia, sometimes most richly decorated.

Brewster-shape. Oval teapot with oval lid and straight sides. Made at the Wedgwood factory in the late 18th century, and at many others.

'Brinjal Bowls'. K'ang Hsi porcelain bowls decorated with yellow and green flower sprays on aubergine purple ground.

Brislington. Delftware factory near Bristol in production from mid-17th to mid-18th century.

Bristol Delftware. Early ware similar to LAMBETH; later, to LIVERPOOL. See also BIANCO-SOPRA-BIANCO.

19

Bristol Porcelain. Early product: soft-paste porcelain. In 1752, amalgamated with Worcester; thenceforward the two products were indistinguishable. In the second period hard-paste porcelain wares ranged from cottage china to elegant services and sets of figures decorated in the Sèvres style.

'Brocaded Imari'. Blue, red and gold porcelain exported from Japan in the first half of the 18th century; inspiration for patterns later produced by Derby, Worcester, Spode, Mintons and Masons.

Brown and Black Glazes. Occur in Sung stonewares; coffee and brown glazes are to be found on Ming porcelain.

'Buckwheat' Celadon Ware. *Tobi seiji*, Japanese name for brown-spotted Sung celadon wares of Lung-chüan.

Bull-baiting Group. Pottery representation of a bull tossing a dog, on base supported by six short legs. Early 19th century.

Bull-baiting group

Burlington (Vermont) Pottery. Early 19th-century pottery started by an Englishman, Norman Judd, from the Bennington Pottery.

Burslem. Largest pottery district in 17th-century England.

Bussa. Cornish earthenware pot for salting down pilchards.

Butter-pot. 17th-century earthenware vessel made at Burslem for holding a 14 lb. measure of butter for marketing.

'C' Mark. Associated with Caughley and Frankenthal porcelain and Clichy paperweights.

Cadogan teapot

Canton Enamel plate

Cabaret Set. Porcelain teaset for one or two people, with porcelain tray.

Cabbage-leaf Jug. Worcester jugs with cylindrical necks and relief-ornamented ovoid bodies, the decoration being super-imposed.

Cadogan Teapot. First made at the end of the 18th century with a purple-brown 'Rockingham' glaze; teapot filled from hole in the base, the inspiration for which was reputed to be a Chinese teapot of this kind imported by the Hon. Mrs Cadogan.

Café-au-Lait Glaze. Colour as the name suggests; found on Chinese porcelain of the Ch'ing dynasty.

Caffaggioli Maiolica. Tin-glazed earthenware made at the Medici castle of Caffaggioli after the 15th century.

Cambrian Pottery. See SWANSEA EARTHENWARE AND PORCELAIN.

Cane Ware. See also 'BAMBOO' WARE. Caneware, on the other hand, was sometimes enamelled in blue and other colours.

Canton Enamel. Exported to England from China in the 18th and 19th centuries; enamel ware on copper decorated in the *famille rose* style.

Canton Porcelain. 19th-century Chinese export to Europe; porcelain with a celadon-green ground, decorated with butterflies, flowers, etc.

'Capacity' Mug. Measure used in ale-houses or by shop-keepers; made in salt-glazed stoneware from the end of the 17th century, in dipped, mocha, and banded earthenware from the end of the 18th century.

Capo-di-Monte Porcelain. Soft-paste porcelain made at Naples in the mid-18th century. Many reproductions exist.

Capo-di-Monte figures

Carpet Balls. Made in brown stoneware or white earthenware, with ringed or flower patterns, used in the Victorian game of carpet bowls.

Cassel Porcelain. 18th-century German tablewares; marked 'H C' (Hesse Cassel) in blue or with heraldic lion of Hesse.

Castel Durante Maiolica. Italian tin-glazed earthenware made from the 16th century.

Castelli Maiolica. Like CASTEL DURANTE maiolica, decorated with mythological or historical scenes. 17th and 18th century.

Castle Hedingham. Site of 19th-century pottery at which 'medieval' and 'Tudor' pottery wares were made.

Castleford Pottery. Established c. 1790. Most characteristic wares, unglazed stoneware with relief decorations in panels.

Examples of Cats

Chantilly Porcelain

'Chantilly sprig'

Caughley Porcelain sauce-boat

'C D' marks on Coalport

Cats. Figures made in striped agate stoneware, earthenware and delftware in the mid-18th century.

Caughley Porcelain. Not dissimilar from Worcester; the 'Willow' and 'Broseley Dragon' patterns originated at the Caughley Works, which was in operation in the second half of the 18th century.

'C D' Mark. A mark of COALPORT PORCELAIN.

Celadon. Willow green. Pale grey-green glaze on Chinese pottery or porcelain.

Chantilly Porcelain. Opaque porcelain made at Chantilly, France, from about 1725. The 'Chantilly sprig', a motif of small blue flowers, was popular and much copied in England.

Chelsea figure

Chelsea-Derby
sugar bowl

Ch'eng Hua Period bowl   Chia Ching Period plate

Chelsea. Porcelain made at a factory in Chelsea, London, from about the mid-18th century.

Chelsea-Derby. When the Chelsea factory was bought by William Duesbury and John Heath of Derby, the Derby styles took precedence over the former Chelsea styles; thence the compromise ascription.

Ch'êng Hua Period. 1465–87. The rarest examples had coloured enamels over thin underglaze blue outlines, a style which had many imitators in the 17th century.

Chesterfield Stoneware. Brown stonewares frequently with hunting scenes or drinking bouts depicted in relief decoration.

Chia Ch'ing Period. 1796–1820. Popular among other products of this period was an iron-red enamelling.

24

Ch'ien Lung Period porcelain

Chia Ching Period. 1522–66. Period of the Ming reign famous for its blue-and-white porcelain of a rich violet tone; also for the development of some brilliantly coloured enamel painting.

Ch'ien Lung Porcelain. 1736–95. The end of the period showed a decline in materials and inspiration. The period as a whole borrowed much from classical styles.

Chien Ware. Brown and black ware made during the Sung dynasty; usually small conical tea-bowls.

Chill. Cornish earthenware oil lamp (using pilchard oil) in the form of a large candlestick.

China-clay. Decomposed felspathic rock; an ingredient of hard-paste porcelain and English bone-china.

'China' Dogs. Earthenware representations of various breeds of dog, particularly popular in Wales and the West Country.

China-stone. Fusible felspathic rock, sometimes known as Cornish stone from its county of origin.

Examples of 'China' dogs

25

Chinese Export Porcelain. Dating from the latter part of the 17th century, when wares began to be manufactured specifically for export. Some designs drawn from European sources; some examples bear coat of arms of purchaser.

Chinese 'Imari'. Early 18th-century imitations of Japanese export porcelain wares.

Chinese Lowestoft. See CHAFFERS, WILLIAM (Craftsmen and Manufacturers).

Ch'ing Dynasty. Period 1644–1912.

Ching-te-Chen. Chinese centre of porcelain industry from the 14th century, in Kiangsi Province.

Chinoiserie. Broad appelation for articles designed in the Chinese style, popular from the 17th to mid-18th century.

Example of Chinoiserie

Chun Ware bowl

Christening Goblet. Four-handled loving cup with whistle attached for attracting attention when it requires to be refilled.

Chun Ware. Sung stoneware, with thick opalescent glaze ranging from pale lavender to deep blue.

Claire-de-Lune Glazes. Lavender blue glazes frequently used on Chinese porcelain.

Claret Ground. Crimson ground colour introduced at the Chelsea factory in 1760.

Clay. Special plastic earths of varying grades and colours, from coarse red-burning clay for bricks and tiles to blue clay for stoneware and white Kaolin for porcelains.

Clobbering. Ineffectual and patched up attempt at applying enamelled decoration to porcelain.

Clover-leaf Mark. Associated with Limbach porcelain from 1786–92 (q.v.).

Coalbrookdale. Factory making terracotta from 1861.

Coalport. Factory started by John Rose, c. 1796, after he had left the Caughley factory (q.v.).

Coalport vase

Coffee Can

Cockpit Hill Pottery. Staffordshire-type ware.

Codnor Park Stoneware. 19th-century manufactory of stoneware bottles from local clay.

Coffee Can. Miniature mug.

Cologne Stoneware. As FULHAM STONEWARE was sometimes known in the 17th century. Semi-translucent stoneware, and earthenware pots and mugs, etc.

Combed Ware. Pottery brushed or combed to resemble in effect marbled paper. Late 17th and early 18th century.

'Compagnie des Indes' China. Chinese porcelain imported into Europe by the French trading company of that name.

Copeland teapot

Pottery cottages

Compagnie Dessin. French name for porcelain made to order in the Far East for European customers and imported by the Compagnie des Indes.

Conture-framing. The use of a border in conjunction with a decorative pattern on pottery.

Copeland. Originally the firm of Spode, acquired in 1833 by William Taylor Copeland.

Copenhagen Porcelain. Soft-paste porcelain made at a factory at Copenhagen from the mid-18th century.

Copper-red Porcelain Glazes. Magnificent high-temperature glazes used in Chinese porcelain; brilliantly executed as early as the 15th century.

Costrel. Pilgrim's bottle, suspended by a sling from ears or handles.

Cottages. Pottery cottages were variously used: as night-light shields, pastille burners, and mantelpiece ornaments.

'Cow' Milk Jug. Model of cow filled through a hole in the back, the mouth and tail forming the spout and handle. Made in silver as well as in pottery. Also called COW CREAMER.

**'Cow' Milk Jug.   Example of Crackleware.   Cream-coloured
Earthenware coffee-pot**

Cozzi Porcelain. Soft-paste porcelain made largely in imitation of Meissen by Geminiano Cozzi in Venice in the second half of the 18th century.

'Cracked Ice' Pattern. Simulation of ice cracks used as a form of decoration on Bristol delftware, c. 1770.

Crackleware. China ware with minute cracks all over the surface. The method by which this effect was achieved was long known by the Chinese, but was not introduced into Europe until the 19th century.

Cradle Pipe-tray. Pottery piece intended as a wedding gift.

Crazing. Fine network of cracks which sometimes appear in the glaze on earthenware due to unequal shrinkage of glaze and body. See CRACKLEWARE for deliberate effect of crazing.

Cream-coloured Earthenware. Good quality tableware, made in Staffordshire, Yorkshire and elsewhere, internationally used in the late 18th and early 19th centuries. Known also as CREAMWARE.

Crescent Mark. Associated with Caughley and Worcester porcelain.

Crich. Derbyshire Crich clay.

Cross Mark. Associated with Bristol, Plymouth and Worcester porcelain.

Crossed 'L's' Mark. Associated with Sèvres, Limbach and Longton Hall porcelain.

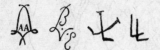

Crossed 'L's' marks. Sèvres, Limbach, Longton Hall

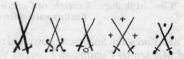

Crossed Swords marks. Two Meissen, Two Tournai, Weesp

Crossed Swords Mark. Associated with Meissen, Tournai and Weesp porcelain.

Crouch Ware. Probably the earliest Staffordshire salt-glazed pottery.

Crown Derby Porcelain. See DERBY PORCELAIN.

'C T' Mark. Associated with Bow porcelain.

Cuckoo. Bird call in shape of large spotted bird perched with four smaller birds on a fence. Mostly made in slipware.

'C V' Mark. Associated with Kloster Veilsdorf porcelain.

Dagger Mark. Associated with Bow porcelain after 1760.

D'Alva Bottles. Also called BELLARMINES.

'Darkie' Toby Jug. As the name suggests, toby jug representing a black man (late 19th century).

Deirdritic. Descriptive of tree-like markings.

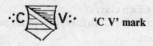

'C V' mark

Delft vase and cover

Derby figure

Delft. Pottery produced at Delft, centre of the Dutch industry, from the mid-17th century; usually with white glaze on which a decoration is painted in blue.

Delftware. Earthenware coated with an opaque lead glaze made in Delft, Holland, from the 17th century. See TIN ENAMELLED EARTHENWARE.

Denby (Derbyshire). Brown stoneware pottery, late 18th and 19th centuries, made by Bourne & Son.

Derby. Soft-paste porcelain was made at Derby from the mid-18th to mid-19th century. In 1876 the present Royal Crown Derby Porcelain Company was formed. Figures formed a large part of the company's production until the Chelsea-Derby period (q.v.) when more attention was paid to useful wares.

Derbyshire Pottery. Includes the slipwares made at Bolsover and Tickenhall; brown salt-glazed stonewares made at Chesterfield, Brampton, Denby, Codnor Park and Belper; cream-colour at Cockpit Hill; and porcelain at Derby.

Deruta Maiolica. Deruta, near Perugia, was particularly famous for its lustred wares dating from the 16th century.

Deutsche Blumen. 'German Flowers.' Naturalistically painted flowers used as decoration on Meissen porcelain, c. 1740.

31

Devonshire Pottery. Pottery made at one or another of several important Devon potteries from the 17th century.

'Dipped' Pottery. On the authority of William Evans, writing in 1846, includes marbled slipware, 'Mocha' and banded wares.

Dishes. Plates upwards of 12 inches diameter.

'D K' Mark. Associated with Derby porcelain.

Doccia Porcelain. Soft- and later, hard-paste porcelain made at a factory at Doccia, Italy, from 1735.

Doccia Porcelain coffee pot

Doulton Porcelain vase

'Doctor Syntax'. The hero of William Coombe's narrative poem, whose adventures were represented in transfer-prints on tableware by James and Ralph Clews at Cobridge, c. 1821.

Don Pottery. White and cream-coloured earthenware, green glazed wares, transfer-printed pottery and other stonewares made at this pottery from the last decade of the 18th century.

Dots Mark. Associated with Bow porcelain.

Doulton Porcelain. From the time of the Battle of Waterloo the firm of Doulton and Watts, as it was first called, expanded steadily into a highly successful business, making a wide range of products from chemical and sanitary items to toby jugs and modelled figures, etc. in a great variety of decorative forms and colour glazes.

Dresden. English name for porcelain made at Meissen, near Dresden.

Drug Jar. Made throughout the 17th and 18th centuries for apothecaries; variously decorated.

Drug Jar

'Drunken Parson' Toby Jug. Subject with hat awry and up-turned beer mug.

Duck Egg Porcelain. Swansea soft-paste porcelain with greenish translucency, made c. 1816–17.

'D V' Mark. Associated with certain examples of Mennecy porcelain.

East India Company China. Imported Chinese porcelain. See COMPAGNIE DES INDES.

Egg Shell Porcelain. 'Egg shell' thin porcelain first made in China, later emulated by such makers as Mintons, Belleek, etc.

Egyptian Black. See BASALTES. 'Dry' black stoneware made by Josiah Wedgwood.

Email Ombrant. Pottery decoration which, in effect, appeared as a monochrome picture in a variety of tones.

En Camaieu. See EMAIL OMBRANT.

Encaustic Tiles. The word encaustic means baked or burnt, and is frequently applied to medieval inlaid tiles and to 19th-century imitations. Red, orange, white, green, blue, yellow and a matt and 'shining' black were produced and used in decoration of basaltes bodies, modelled and painted in imitation of ancient Greek ware. Wedgwood took out a patent in 1769 for 'ornamenting earthen and porcelaine ware with an encaustic gold bronze . . . in imitation of the ancient Etruscan and Roman earthenware'.

Engine Turning. Method of producing various patterns on an unfired pot (e.g. geometrical, fluted, etc.) by turning on a specially designed lathe.

Examples of Engine Turning

Engobe. Liquid clay applied as coating to pottery.

Erect Thumbpiece. Found on early 17th-century pewter flagons.

Etruria. Name given to a village which Wedgwood planned on the Ridge House Estate where, with his work-people, he sought to revive the lost art of the Etruscans.

European-style Decoration. 18th-century Chinese porcelain decorated to order with European heraldic emblems and print subjects.

'F' and F reversed Mark. Associated with Worcester, Fürstenberg, Fulda and Medici porcelain.

'Fable' Painter. Unknown artist who decorated table wares with illustrations taken from the folio edition of *Aesop's Fables* (1687), by Francis Barlow.

Faenza Maiolica. Many devotional figures in imitation of enamelled terracotta were made from the 15th century.

Faience. French name for painted or glazed earthenware maiolica.

'Fair Hebe' Jug. On one side of the jug (which is in the form of a tree) is modelled a young man handing to a girl seated below the tree a nest of eggs; above is a legend reading 'Fair Hebe'. On the other side is a man with a glass in hand; the legend reads 'A Bumper'.

'Fair Hebe' jug   Famille Rose lion

Fair Toxophilite. See 'FEMALE ARCHER'.

Famille Rose. Chinese enamelled porcelain wares of the reigns of Yung Chêng and Ch'ien Lung. The rose-pink which gave it its name was introduced from Europe. FAMILLE VERTE and FAMILLE NOIRE belong to the K'ang Hsi period, the former being distinguished for its brilliant green and strong iron-red, the latter by the green glaze which covers the dry black ground. FAMILLE JAUNE is so named for its yellow ground.

Fazackerley Flowers. Delftware with strong floral ornamentation in green, dark blue, brick red and bright yellow said to have been made about the middle of the 18th century for a certain Thomas Fazackerley.

'F B B' Mark. Associated with Worcester porcelain.

35

Feathered Ware. See COMBED WARE.

Feeding Bottle. A flattened, oval-shaped article with small aperture and nozzle at top.

Felspar China. Felspathic china made c. 1820 by the younger Josiah Spode and so identified by transfer-print.

Felspathic Glazes. Those having felspar rock content; used on porcelain and earthenware.

'Female Archer'. Satirical jibe at the fashion of the time; subject for jugs and earthenware figures.

Ferruginous. Containing iron rust or iron as a chemical constituent; reddish-brown in colour.

Ferrybridge. Pottery near Pontefract, Yorkshire, run by Ralph Wedgwood's partner, which made Wedgwood-style stoneware and creamware in the late 18th and early 19th century.

Fiddler Jug. Early toby jug representing seated figure playing fiddle.

Figure Jugs. See TOBY JUGS.

Fitzhugh. Name said to be American bastardisation of Foochow. Chinese floral pattern comprising centre medallions of flowers and emblems (in underglaze blue and overglaze green, brown and orange) with border of pomegranates, butterflies and lattice work.

Flambé Glazes. Found on Chinese ceramics; colour variations produced by kiln conditions.

Flasks. Commonly made in brown stoneware or 'Rockingham' glazed earthenware in the early 19th century. Took a wide variety of forms, from a mermaid, horse pistol, or cubercum to the figure of a royal person or celebrated politician.

Flint Enamel. A refined version of brown 'Rockingham' glaze (q.v.), patented in America in the mid-19th century and later copied in England.

'Florentine Green' Dishes. Product of Florence in the mid-15th century; maiolica dishes painted in green, orange and purple.

Flowers. Adornments to porcelain figures, usually mounted on ormolu branches; made in Chelsea and Derby.

Flown Blue Decoration. Method of decorating porcelain, much in vogue in Victorian times, by which the design merges into the surrounding glaze to produce a sort of coloured halo effect.

Food Warmer. Hollow pedestal, 9 to 12 inches high, with side opening and internal cup or container and surmounting covered bowl. 18th and 19th century.

Food Warmer   Typical Fuddling-cup   Fulda Porcelain group

Frankenthal Porcelain. Made near Mannheim, in Germany, from 1755–99. Tablewares sometimes decorated in the Meissen manner.

'Fretted Square' Mark. Associated with Worcester porcelain.

Fuddling-cup. Combination cup with 3, 5, 6 or more 'compartments', the liquid content running freely from one to another, made in sgraffito slipware. Earliest examples date from the first half of the 17th century.

Fukien Porcelain. See BLANC-DE-CHINE.

Fulda Porcelain. A hard-paste porcelain made in Germany from 1764–90.

Fulham Stoneware mug.   Fürstenberg Porcelain figure.   Figures
in Gardner's Porcelain

Fulham Stoneware. Made by John Dwight (q.v.) and family.
Dwight was the first maker of semi-translucent stoneware.

Fürstenberg Porcelain. Founded in 1747, the Fürstenberg
factory produced classical figures and copies of Wedgwood's
jasper and black basaltes ware.

'G' Mark. Associated with Gotha, Limbach and Berlin
porcelain.

Gallipots. For the most part, small, glazed earthenware pots
such as were used for ointments.

Gally Paving Tiles. Glazed tiles used for wall decorations.
Origin of name: wares brought from the Mediterranean in
galleys.

Gardner's Porcelain. Gardner was an Englishman who founded
a factory in Moscow about the middle of the 18th century;
he employed the Russian peasant as a subject for many of his
figures. Also called MOSCOW PORCELAIN.

Garnish. Household set of plates and dishes.

Gaudy Dutch. American name for a brightly decorated
Staffordshire pottery made for the American market early in
the 19th century.

Gaudy Welsh. American name for English pottery made for the American market in the decade or so before and after the mid-19th century. Also called GAUDY IRONSTONE.

German Flowers. See DEUTSCHE BLUMEN.

Gera Porcelain. See LIMBACH PORCELAIN.

Giobu. Japanese lacquer-work technique, giving a mottled effect.

Glaze. A shiny coating applied to porcelain to render it proof against liquids and to give it a smooth surface.

Globular. Globe-shaped, spherical; composed of globules.

'Goat and Bee' Jug. Jug decorated with goats and a bee in relief. These jugs were made at Coalport about the middle of the 19th century.

'Goat and Bee' jug

Godet. A drinking cup; c. 1630.

Gold Anchor Mark. Associated with Chelsea porcelain.

Gold Star. In popular use as border for tea and dinner services at the end of the 18th and beginning of the 19th century.

Gombron Ware. Gombron (now Bandar Abbas), port in the Persian Gulf, from which Persian ware and Chinese porcelain were imported into England in the 18th century.

Gotch. East Anglian term for a large stoneware jug.

Gotha Porcelain. Vases in the classical manner, figures, etc., made in Gotha, Germany, in the second half of the 18th century.

Granite Ware. Cheap, durable white earthenware made for the American market in the mid-19th century.

Gretna Green. Known also as 'The Red Hot Marriage'; black-print depicting runaway couple being married by the Gretna Green blacksmith—accompanied by a verse tag.

Grey Hen. Stoneware liquor bottle.

| Gretna Green print | 'Griffin' mark |

Grey Beard. A BELLARMINE.

'Greyhound' Jug. Jug with greyhound handles and sporting subjects in relief decoration.

'Griffin' Mark. Associated with Rockingham earthenware and porcelain.

Gros Bleu. Ground on stoneware vase.

Grossbreitenbach Porcelain. Made at a factory acquired by the Limbach porcelain company in 1782.

Ground-colours. Coloured glaze area serving as background to painting or gilt decoration on porcelain or enamels.

Grubbe Plates. Source of identity of wares made by the porcelain decorator, James Giles, in the shape of four plates presented to the Victoria and Albert Museum by a Mrs Dora Grubbe, a descendant of Giles.

Gubbio Maiolica (Italy). The Gubbio workshop was celebrated in the 16th century for its lustre wares.

Guernsey Measure. Pewter measure with heart-shaped lid and twin-acorn thumbpiece. Particularly associated with Guernsey, in the Channel Islands.

Han Dynasty vase

Hague, The, Porcelain. Hard-paste porcelain made at The Hague from the third quarter of the 18th century; identification mark is a stork in blue.

Han Dynasty. Embraces the period 206 BC to AD 220. Evidence exists of a considerable mastery of pottery-making techniques during the reign of the Chinese Han Emperors.

Hard-paste Porcelain. True porcelain manufactured from china clay and china stone, glazed with china stone made fusible with a flux.

'HC' Mark. Associated with Cassel porcelain.

'HD' Mark. Associated with Kelsterbach porcelain.

Hearty Good Fellow. A type of toby jug; jovial figure holding a jug.

Hen Dish. Dish in the form of a basket surmounted by sitting hen.

Herculaneum jug

Hoechst porcelain figures

Example of Hollow-ware

Herculaneum. Liverpool pottery founded late 18th century. Produced blue-printed earthenware, cream-coloured stoneware jugs, and porcelain of the Staffordshire type.

Hispano-Moresque Maiolica. Tin-glazed earthenware first made by Moorish craftsmen at Granada; from the 14th to the 17th century at Valencia.

Historical Blue. Also known as 'old blue'. Staffordshire pottery decorated with transfer prints of well-known places, people, events. The deep blue used in the 1820s graduated to a lighter blue in the '30s and '40s.

Hoechst Porcelain. German hard-paste porcelain made from the mid-18th century. Early wares of the Meissen type.

Ho-Ho Bird. Or fêng-huang, meaning phoenix.

Hollow-ware. Vessels made to contain liquid.

42

Honan Ware. Black- and brown-glazed ware of the Sung dynasty, probably made in Honan province.

Horn Mark. Imitation from Chantilly, made at Worcester and Caughley.

Hsüan Tê Period (1426–35). Great period of the 'blue-and-white' Chinese porcelain. Many of the fine wares made at this time were copied centuries later.

Hull, Belle Vue Pottery. Potworks started at the beginning of the 19th century; exported many wares to Germany.

'i' Mark. The mark, from 1792, of Ilmenau porcelain. Ilmenau had been acquired by Limbach six years earlier.

Ilmenau Porcelain. The Ilmenau works was acquired by the firm of Limbach, porcelain makers, in 1786.

'Image' Toys. Name given at the time to mid-18th-century Staffordshire figures.

Imari Porcelain. 'Brocaded Imari' was the inspiration for the later 'Japans' of Derby, Worcester, Spode, Mintons and Masons. See also ARITA PORCELAIN.

Impasto. Thick application of colour in painting. The effect is one of relief.

Incised Decoration on Pottery. Decoration cut into body with sharp instrument.

Example of Honan Ware. Hsüan Tê period bowl. Imari Porcelain bottle

Independent Decorators. In the 18th and 19th centuries independent enamellers and gilders frequently bought porcelain 'in the white' to decorate and sell themselves.

'India' Ware. 18th-century name for imported Chinese porcelain (from East India Company, the importers).

Inlaid Tiles. A form of tile decoration achieved by impressing the body of the tile with punches or printer's types and filling in with a clay of contrasting colour. Used by medieval potters, the application was extended by Sussex potters, c. 1790–1850, to numerous useful and ornamental wares.

Iron Red. Red pigment made from an oxide of iron; used for ceramic decoration.

'Ironstone China' vestibule vase

'Ironstone China'. Produced experimentally, 1740–43, by Andrew Duche at Savannah, and patented in 1813 by C. J. M. Mason of Lane Delph (Staffordshire and Liverpool). Heavy grade, commonly blue printed or painted with 'Japan' patterns. Made in America, 1860–1900, and variously known as white granite, opaque porcelain, flint china (including hotel china and service porcelain, 1885 onwards).

Isleworth Earthenware. Main products: 'Welsh' wares, domestic wares decorated in zig-zag patterns of brown and yellow slip (from c. 1760–1825).

Isnik Pottery. Turkish earthenware made at Isnik in Anatolia from about the middle of the 16th century.

'Istoriato' Painting. Pictorial painting, covering the whole plate. Associated with Urbino (q.v.).

Italian Comedy Figures. Bow and Chelsea porcelain, and Staffordshire salt-glazed wares, having as their subject characters from the *Commedia dell' Arte* (Pierrot, Pantaloon, Harlequin and Columbine, etc.).

Italian Comedy figure (pierrot).   Examples of 'Japans'

Jacobite Pottery. Name given to examples of pottery bearing an inscription or emblem indicating Jacobite sympathies.

'Japans'. Or 'Japan' patterns. Generic term used loosely to comprehend a wide range of oriental patterns and styles used in the decoration of English porcelain in the 18th and 19th centuries (including the Chinese *famille verte* and *famille rose* patterns). Extensively used in the 1820s on Spode, Minton and Davenport bone china.

Jasper. Wedgwood described it as 'white porcelain *bisque* of exquisite beauty and delicacy'. Not to be confused with 'Jasper dip', a coloured solution into which the white jasper body was dipped; also a white jasper ware covered with a surface colouring.

Jasper medallion

'Jesuit' China plate

Jasper Dip. Coloured solution applied to white jasper body by dipping. Jasperware was a fine-grained unglazed stoneware prefected by Wedgwood in 1775 and subsequently copied by many others.

Jaune Jonquille. Daffodil-yellow enamel ground used on Sèvres porcelain.

'Jesuit' China. 18th-century Chinese porcelain wares decorated with Christian subjects, the references being supplied by Jesuit missionaries.

Jet-enamelled Ware. Celebrated 18th-century Worcester porcelain wares transfer-printed in black.

Jidai. Early period piece of Japanese lacquer-work.

Johanneum. Building in Dresden housing the porcelain collection of King Frederick Augustus the Strong of Saxony. Inventory marks dating back to 1721 provide clues to the identification of the types of porcelain, which include Chinese and Japanese stoneware.

Joney or Joney Grig. Dialect description of a pottery chimney ornament in the shape of a dog.

Ju Ware. Rare, early 12th-century Imperial Chinese porcelain ware.

Ju-I. Decorative motif on certain types of Chinese porcelain; a sceptre with cloud-scroll head, emblem of fulfilled wishes.

Kakiemon Style. Distinctive style of decoration used on Japanese porcelain, widely imitated by the Germans, French and English in the 18th century. See also ARITA PORCELAIN.

K'ang Hsi Porcelain. Emperor K'ang Hsi (1662–1722) reigned during one of the noblest periods of Chinese porcelain design and decoration.

Kaolin. See CHINA CLAY.

'Keep Within Compass'. Emblem of morality used by John Aynesley (1752–1829) as decorative motif on earthenware—depicting the rewards of virtue and the punishments of sin.

Kelsterbach Porcelain. Hard-paste porcelain made at the factory of the Landgrave of Hesse-Darmstadt, Ludwig VIII, from 1761.

Kick. A dent in the shape of a pyramid found in the bases of many bowls, bottles and glass decanters made prior to 1760.

Kiln. Oven in which hard-paste porcelain body and glaze is fired at a temperature of 1200°–1400° C.

Kiln Waster. Spoilt porcelain from the kiln.

Kakiemon Style dish

K'ang Hsi Porcelain vase

'Kinuta' Celadon Ware. See LUNG-CHÜAN CELADON WARE.

Kloster Veilsdorf Porcelain. Hard-paste porcelain made in Thuringia from 1760.

Ko Ware. Crackled Sung celadon ware of Kuan type.

'KPM' Mark. Associated with Meissen porcelain in the first quarter of the 18th century.

Ko Ware vase   'KPM' mark   Kuan Ware vase

Ku Yueh Hsuan Ware. 18th-century Imperial quality Chinese porcelain wares with flower and landscape decorations and, frequently, with a poetic inscription.

Kuan Ware. Rare, 12th-century Chinese celadon copied during the 18th century, employing crackled glaze with an effect resembling marble or jade.

'L' Mark. Associated with Worcester and Longton Hall porcelain.

Lambeth Delftware. Delftware and maiolica, examples of which date back to the late 16th century.

Lang Yao. The first productions of the reign of K'ang Hsi (1662–1722) were the famous green and blood-red Lang Yao glazes (classified in the *sang de boeuf* group), made in an attempt to reproduce the glazes of the potters of earlier times.

Lazulite. Blue-tinted parian ware.

Lead Glass. Glass containing lead as a flux. Lead for glazing could be obtained in dry powder form (galena, native lead sulphide) or in liquid form (litterage, lead oxide).

Leeds Earthenware. Manufactured from about 1760. Plates, centrepieces, dishes and figures were fashioned with great skill, many of them being complex in design.

Limbach Porcelain. Porcelain made at a factory in Thuringia owned by the Greiner family from 1772; inexpensive 'utility' wares for the most part. The family owned, in addition, six other porcelain factories in Thuringia. See 'i' MARK.

Lambeth Delftware plate

Leeds Earthenware jug

Limehouse. Porcelain factory manufacturing prior to the mid-18th century. Production remains unidentified.

Ling Lung. Pierced openwork found on a number of 17th- to 18th-century Chinese blue-and-white porcelain bowls; also on certain vases of the Ch'ien Lung and later periods.

Lithophanes. Sometimes called transparencies. Process invented by Baron de Bourgoing in 1827 for the production of

Lithophane decoration

monochrome illusionist pictures by the transmission of light to porcelain or bone china transparencies moulded thinly in *intaglio*.

Liverpool Delftware. The manufacture of delftware began in Liverpool in 1710, but had almost ceased by 1780 when many of the best potters had migrated to Staffordshire.

Liverpool Porcelain. Made in great variety, of a soft, heavy and somewhat coarse paste, with a bluish glaze often deepening towards the base. Typical articles are tall jugs and coffee-pots, and barrel-shaped mugs. Some pieces can well be mistaken for Worcester.

Liverpool Pottery (Creamware). Pottery founded in 1793–4; re-named 'Herculaneum' in 1796. Made creamware transfer-

Liverpool Porcelain jar

Longton Hall bowl

printed in blue or black, and other Staffordshire-type wares. In America the name Liverpool was accorded to all cream-ware made in Liverpool between 1780 and 1825, also to the work of the Staffordshire potters, especially jugs in black, transfer-printed with American historical subjects.

'Long Elizas'. Chinese women represented in strangely elongated form found on Worcester porcelain in the 1760s.

Longton Hall Porcelain. First porcelain factory in Staffordshire. Earlier examples are notable for their heavy yet translucent quality; later, finer examples for their imitation of Meissen.

Lowestoft Porcelain plate

Ludwigsburg Porcelain figure

Lotus Ware. Name given to a version of BELLEEK (q.v.), produced in America, 1882–1900.

'Lowdin's' Bristol. A type of soft-paste porcelain made at Bristol about the mid-18th century at a glasshouse owned by William Lowdin and known as Lowdin's China House.

Lowestoft Porcelain. In the second half of the 18th century coloured and blue-and-white ware was produced, to be followed in the later period by a variety of tablewares and commemorative pieces.

Ludwigsburg Porcelain. Hard-paste porcelain factory near

51

Stuttgart operating in the second half of the 18th century and into the 19th. Notable for its figures.

'Lund's' Bristol. See 'LOWDIN'S' BRISTOL, of which William Miller and Benjamin Lund were the makers. They appear to be identical.

'Lund's' Bristol jug

Lung-chüan Celadon Ware. Lung-chüan was a flourishing centre for celadon wares in the Sung dynasty. Notable are the Kinuta celadon and the Japanese tobi seiji.

Lustre Colour. Found on early Meissen porcelain, as background for painted designs or for overglaze marks. Pale mother-of-pearl shade with an element of red.

Lustre Decoration. Irridescent glaze applied to pottery or porcelain by means of thin films of metal.

'M' Mark. Associated with Minton porcelain.

Lung-chüan Celadon ware.   **'M' mark.**   **Lustre decorated jug**

Maiolica jug

'Malling' jug

Marbled Ware mug

Maiolica. Tin-glazed earthenware made in Spain and Italy from the 14th century. Term later applied to all earthenware with painted decoration on tin glaze. Not to be confused with Majolica, the name given by Victorian potters to coloured glazed earthenware introduced by Mintons in the mid-18th century and to a wide range of decorated pottery from architectural pottery to umbrella stands.

Malachite. Parian ware coloured to resemble the green malachite stone.

'Malling' Jugs. English tin-glazed pottery (name derived from an example found in West Malling church, Kent) mottled in imitation of Rhenish 'Tigerwares'.

Manchu Dynasty. Dynasty of the Ch'ing emperors in China (1644–1912).

Mandarin. Late 18th-century decoration. Groups of figures in official dress painted in panels bordered by various decorative patterns. See MANDARIN CHINA.

'Mandarin' China. Imported from China during the second half of the 18th century. Floral or figure subjects, for the most part, enamelled in pink, red and gold, frequently framed in underglaze blue scrollwork.

Marbled Ware. Marbled earthenwares were made in China

during the T'ang and Sung dynasties. See also COMBED WARE.

Marienberg Porcelain. Made near Stockholm from c. 1766.

Marks. Signs of origin of porcelain, usually indicating factory, painter or 'repairer'; sometimes a warehouse sign. Marks are executed in underglaze blue or are impressed, incised or

Martha Gunn Toby jug.   Medici Porcelain jug.   Mei P'ing
'prunus' vase

painted above glaze. They usually appear on the base of an article, but sometimes form a part of the pattern.

Martha Gunn. Toby jug in representation of an 18th-century Brighton character, Martha Gunn, the bathing-woman.

Mason's Bone China. Made at Fenton, Staffordshire, from 1800 to 1854, notably blue-printed earthenware and a quantity of ironstone china pieces. Much use was made of Imari patterns and pseudo-Chinese decorations.

Matt Glaze. Glaze with non-reflective surface.

Mazarine Blue. Dark, rich blue used for decoration of porcelain.

'M B' Mark. Associated with Marienberg porcelain.

Medici Porcelain. Made at Florence, c. 1560, under the

patronage of Francesco de' Medici; marked the first successful attempt to make porcelain in Europe.

Medium and Low Temperature Glazes. Medium temperature glazes refer to certain coloured glazes applied to the baked biscuit and afterwards re-fired at medium temperature (e.g. Ming 3-colour class). Low temperature glazes are associated with the more familiar enamels of overglaze painting fired in the 'muffle kiln' in a wide variety of shades and in most colours of *famille verte* and *famille rose*—usually opaque.

Meissen figure and coffee-pot   **Mennecy Porcelain jar**

Mei P'ing. Chinese porcelain 'prunus' vase designed to hold single spray of plum-blossom.

Meissen. The Meissen factory, near Dresden, the earliest European porcelain factory, was founded in 1710. The 19th-century versions of original Meissen wares are commonly known as 'Dresden'.

Mennecy Porcelain. Soft-paste porcelain made at Mennecy, Ile-de-France, 1735–85. Tea-ware, coffee- and flower-pots, and vases were the main products. Also called Bourg-la-Reine.

'Merryman' Plates. Set of six tin-glazed earthenware plates made from last quarter of 17th century to the mid-18th century, bearing rhymes and inscriptions conveying worthy and moral sentiments.

Metropolitan Slipware. Jugs, mugs, bowls, chamber-pots, etc. dating from before the mid-17th century in red earthenware, sometimes bearing Puritan inscriptions.

Midshipman Jug. Early variety of toby jug.

Mille Fleurs. Chinese porcelain decoration; panels of growing plants on flower-covered ground.

| Ming Dynasty vase | 'Merryman' plate | Minton jar |

Ming Dynasty. Period 1368 to 1644. Examples of Ming porcelain are exceedingly rare with exception of exported blue-and-white and the 'Transitional' wares brought to Europe after 1600.

Minton Porcelain. Factory founded by Thomas Minton in 1793. Table wares have always represented a large part of their output.

'M L' Mark. Associated with Weesp porcelain.

Mocha Ware. Form of 'dipped' pottery. Process used from about 1780–1914 and chiefly applied to ale and other measures.

Mocha Ware jug   **Examples of Money Boxes**

Moco, Moko. Cheap 19th-century substitute for Mocha ware. Buff or red ware mottled with various colours, splashed over the article before glazing.

Money Boxes. Made from medieval times of pottery in a variety of shapes, from houses and chests of drawers to pigs, hens and chickens.

Monkey Orchestra. Figure group listed in the Chelsea catalogue of 1756; copied from a series of Meissen figures.

Monochrome-glazed Porcelain. Made in white, blue, copper-red, celadon-green, and brown or black with high temperature glazes fired in one process; also in medium and low-temperature colours.

Monkey Orchestra figures

'**Moonlight' Lustre.** Colours used, particularly by Wedgwood in the early 19th century, in such a way as to produce on earthenware a marbled lustre effect.

'**Moons'.** Patches of extra translucency to be found on some early porcelain when held to the light.

Moscow Porcelain. See GARDNER'S PORCELAIN.

Moustache-cup. Victorian piece; cup with device to shield moustache from contact with liquid.

Moustiers Faience. Moustiers, in Provence, was a centre of the faience trade in the 18th century.

'Mr and Mrs Caudle' flask

'Moonlight' Lustre wall pocket

'**Mr and Mrs Caudle'.** Characters from Douglas Jerrold's *Mrs Caudle's Curtain Lectures* represented as relief decoration on Doulton brown stoneware spirit flasks about the mid-19th century.

Muffle Kiln. Kiln used for low temperature firing (700°–900° C.). The muffle is an inner chamber, the repository of the porcelain, protected from the flames and smoke of the kiln. Used for firing soft paste and enamel painting into the glaze of faience and porcelain.

'**N' Mark.** Associated with New Hall porcelain.

'**Nankin' China.** Blue and white porcelain of the late 18th and 19th century imported from Nanking.

Nantgarw Porcelain jar   **'New Canton' inkwell**

'Nankin Yellow'. Glaze used in conjunction with K'ang Hsi underglaze blue painting.

Nantgarw Porcelain. Founded in 1813, the Nantgarw factory, near Cardiff, concentrated mostly on table wares, the porcelain being of an unusual translucency.

Neale, James, Earthenware Manufactory. Operating in the last quarter of the 18th century, produced figures of high quality, tableware and vases in the manner of Wedgwood, etc.

'New Canton'. The name under which the merchant firm of Weatherby & Crowther took over the Bow porcelain factory in the mid-18th century.

New Hall Porcelain. Included painted and gilded wares, but, more notably, porcelain decorated with the 'sprigged muslin' type of pattern.

Newcastle-on-Tyne. The St Anthony's pottery and the St

New Hall teapot

Nottingham Earthenware jug.   Nymphenburg Porcelain figure

Peter's pottery produced an inferior kind of creamware from 1781 onwards and 1817 onwards respectively.

Newcastle-under-Lyme Earthenware. Best known for its clay pipes in the 17th century.

Niderviller Porcelain. Product of the French hard-paste porcelain factory established in 1754, distinguished for its figures (e.g. the *Cries of Paris*).

'Night-Watchman' Jug. Toby jug representing figure holding hat and lantern.

Northern Celadon. Chinese Sung wares thought to originate from Honan Province.

Nottingham Earthenware. Pottery was made in Nottingham from the 13th century until about 1800. Examples of salt-glazed articles are notable for their fine and assured workmanship.

Nove Porcelain. Venetian porcelain made from about 1752.

Nymphenburg Porcelain. Manufactured from the mid-18th century, renowned for the figures modelled by Franz Anton Bustelli.

Nyon Porcelain. Made at Nyon, near Geneva, from 1780 to 1813.

'Oak-leaf Jars'. Mid-15th-century Tuscan drug-jars decorated with foliage in impasto-flue.

Obsidian. Glassy, volcanic rock with dark green flecks; parian ware was frequently made in imitation of obsidian in the mid-19th century.

Oeil-de-Perdrix. Decoration of small circles on porcelain.

Oil-gilding. Gilding by use of japanner's size.

'Oilspot' Glaze. Silvery spots on certain Chinese wares, the result of precipitated iron crystals.

On-glaze Decoration. Decoration to porcelain or pottery applied over the glaze.

Opalescent Enamel. Semi-transparent enamel.

Opaque China. Trade name for a white porcelain-type earthenware used by Swansea, Ridgway & Morley and others.

Oeil-de-Perdrix decoration

'Orange-jumper'. Local character attired in orange employed as subject on Yorkshire cream-coloured earthenware made at the Don pottery, c. 1808.

Ostrich Egg Cup. Ostrich eggs were often mounted as cups in the 16th century and later.

Ottweiler Porcelain Factory. German factory operating from 1763 to 1797, first making hard-paste porcelain and then earthenware.

Oude Amstal Porcelain. Oude Amstal was the location of the Dutch Weesp porcelain works from 1784.

Oude Loosdrecht Porcelain. Oude Loosdrecht was the location of the Weesp porcelain factory from 1771 to 1784.

Overglaze. Decoration to porcelain or pottery applied above the glaze.

Owl jug   **Typical Pap Boat**   **Parian Ware figure**

Owl Jugs. Slipware and white salt-glazed stoneware jugs with detachable heads made successively from the late 17th to late 18th century.

Ox-blood Glaze. Famous Chinese porcelain glaze known as *sang de boeuf*.

Palissy Ware. Lead-glazed pottery made in the 16th century by Bernard Pallisy, decorated with casts from nature of fishes, reptiles, etc.

Pancheon. Shallow bowl used for settling milk.

Pap Boat. Shallow dish with spout, for feeding infants.

Parian Ware. Special biscuit porcelain used for statuary and elaborately moulded wares, evolved in the late 1840s, possessing a delicate smear-glazed surface.

'Parson and Clerk'. Earthenware figure group consisting of drunken parson assisted by his clerk.

Parting-shards. Thin bits of old pottery used to divide newly made pots after they have been glazed to prevent them from sticking together.

'Patch' Family. Chelsea and Derby figures having unglazed patches on their under-surface, the result of their having been rested on pads of clay during the glost (lead glaze) firing.

Pâte-sur-pâte. French process, first practised at Sèvres, of building up translucent white or tinted reliefs on coloured parian or porcelain by modelling or painting.

'Paul Pry'. John Poole's hero as subject of toby jug.

'Peachbloom' Glazes. Rare brownish-pink Chinese porcelain glaze.

Pear Shape. Curved or pyriform shape in hollow-ware.

'Pearl' Ware. White earthenware with higher proportion of flint and white clay than cream-coloured ware.

Peasant Style. Earthenware ornament painted in the 'resist' lustre style. The resist is a composition applied to the surface of the article which, when fired away, leaves a white decoration against a bright metallic background.

'Pebbled' Vases. Having marbled surfaces.

Peever. A piece of slate or stone used in the game of hop-scotch, also a disc of pottery used for the same purpose and coloured and lettered with the owner's name. Of 19th-century Scottish origin.

'Peggy Plumper'. Vulgar earthenware decoration depicting domestic tiff between Peggy Plumper and Sammy Spar.

Peking Bowls. Chinese porcelain bowls of Ch'ien Lung period and later.

'Parson and Clerk'   Pâte-sur-pâte panel   'Pearl' Ware figure

'Pew' Group

'Pelican In Her Piety'. Used in Staffordshire slipware. Christian emblem derived from the ancient fallacy that a pelican feeds her young with her own blood.

Petuntse. Generally known as a china-stone, or Cornish stone, since it is quarried in Cornwall. Used in the manufacture of porcelain.

'Pew' Group. Figure group, in white salt-glazed stoneware, or more rarely in earthenware, usually of a man and a woman seated on a high-backed settle (examples of two men and a woman).

'Piatto da Pompa'. Highly decorated ornamental dish.

Pie-crust Ware. Pottery pie dishes with covers modelled as pastry crust.

Pie-crust Ware

Pierced Earthenware

Pilgrim Bottle

Pierced Earthenware. Earthenware hand-pierced with intricate designs.

Pilchard Pots. Made in the West Country for the use of fishermen, in graded sizes.

Pilgrim Bottles. Flattened earthenware (as well as silver and leather) bottles with loops for suspension cords.

Pill-slabs. Made in tin-glazed earthenware, often decorated with the arms of the Apothecaries' Company or of the City of London.

Pineapple Cups. Standing cups in the likeness of the fruit, made in Germany in the 16th and 17th centuries.

'Pineapple' Ware. Green and yellow glazed earthenware, made by Whieldon, Wedgwood and others, in the likeness of pine-

Pill-slab

'Pineapple' Ware teapot

Pinxton Porcelain vase

Plymouth Porcelain cup and saucer

apples, and of cauliflowers and other vegetables. Dates from the mid-18th century.

Pinxton Porcelain. Product of small Derbyshire porcelain factory established towards the end of the 18th century. Cornflower or forget-me-not on white ground is a distinctive Pinxton decoration.

Pipe-clay. White clay used for making tobacco pipes.

Pipkin. Like a small saucepan, made of metal earthenware and used for warming brandy.

Pirlie-pig. Earthenware money-box (from the North Country 'pig' meaning earthen jar, and 'pirlie' something of little value).

'Pistol' Handle. Porcelain or stoneware handles are found in the shape of a pistol handle on many 18th-century knives.

Pitcher Mould. Fired clay mould.

Plique-À-Jour Enamelling. Translucent enamel applied in honeycomb of cells which, when exposed to light, gives effect of stained-glass.

Plymouth Earthenware. Coarse brown and yellow earthenware manufactured at Plymouth in the 18th century. Later, printed or cream colour.

Plymouth Porcelain. First English hard-paste factory, established in 1768. Most of the designs are derivative.

Pontipool. Japanned metal from Birmingham and South Staffordshire was marketed under the name of 'Fancy Pontipool Ware'.

Pontypool Ware. Japanned ware made by the Allgood family at Pontypool, Monmouthshire, from 1730.

Pope and Devil Cup. Reversible cup showing the Pope one way up and the devil the other.

Porcelain. First used, in the 17th and 18th centuries, to describe white wares decorated in the oriental manner; since then, the term has been applied to translucent wares made in imitation of Chinese and Continental porcelain.

Porcelain Transparencies. See LITHOPHANES.

Porphyry Ware. Red-stained parian ware made in the likeness of porphyry (hard rock anciently quarried in Egypt, composed of crystals of white or red felspar in red ground-mass).

Portland House. Wedgwood and Bentley's showroom in Greek Street, opened in 1774.

Portland (or Barberini) Vase. Wedgwood first copied the famous vase, which many believe to have been made at Alexandria about 50 B.C., between 1786 and 1790. The first edition consisted of 29 specimens; there were several subsequent editions.

Wedgwood's Portland Vase

'Portobello' Ware. Pottery made at Tunstall, Staffordshire, in imitation of ware made at Portobello, Scotland.

Posset-pot. Posset was a drink made of hot milk curded with ale, wine, etc., often flavoured with spices, etc., much used as a remedy for colds in the 17th and 18th centuries. The pot, intended to carry posset, was made of stoneware, slipware, delftware, etc., had multiple loop handles and spouts and a dome-shaped lid.

Posset-pot

'Pratt' Ware figure

Potiche. Large Chinese porcelain baluster-shaped jar with cover.

Pottery. Opaque, fired earthenware.

Pottery Figures. Tomb burial figures; large representations of Buddhist apostle, etc.

Pottery Moulds. Several materials were in use in earlier times for the making of moulds; the greatest advance was the introduction about the middle of the 18th century of the porous plaster-of-Paris moulds.

Pottle-pot. Quart pot.

Powder Blue Glaze. Mottled glaze used on Chinese porcelain of the K'ang Hsi period.

'Powdered' (soufflé) Blue. K'ang Hsi period. Used as a surround for underglaze blue or *famille verte* enamel painting, and having gilded designs. Effected by blowing a dry pigment through a tube.

Transfer printing: typical border

Puzzle jug

'Pratt' Ware. Late 18th- and early 19th-century ware decorated with metallic oxide colours capable of withstanding the high-temperature glazing process.

Printing. First found on Battersea porcelain, 1753. Transfer printing on porcelain by means of inking engraved plate.

Puzzle Jug. Common in the 17th and 18th centuries. 'Trick' jug with variety of outlets which the drinker had to stop up in order to imbibe without spilling and thus win the challenge.

Quail Pattern. Bow, Chelsea and Worcester borrowed the pattern from a Japanese Kakiemon example of porcelain ware decorated with two quails in background of rock and foliage.

Queen's Pattern. Also known as the 'Catherine wheel', 'Whorl' or 'Spiral' pattern. Worcester porcelain decoration composed of alternate bands of red-on-white and white-on-blue with gilded embellishments.

Queen's Ware. Name given by Josiah Wedgwood to his

Quail Pattern

cream-coloured earthenware following the receipt of the Queen's patronage.

'R' Mark. Associated with Gotha, Rauenstein and Volkstedt porcelain.

Rauenstein Porcelain. The Rauenstein factory, founded in 1783, was a part of the Limbach 'empire'.

Red Anchor Mark. Associated with Chelsea porcelain.

Red China. Fine red stoneware made in Staffordshire from the late 17th century to the end of the 18th.

Red Glazes and Enamels. Considerable use of these glazes and enamels was made in the Ming period, in K'ang Hsi *famille verte* and some *famille rose*; also as a monochrome glaze for Yung Chêng porcelain. The distinction should be noted between the copper-red glazes and underglaze pigment and the vermilion toned iron-red enamels.

Redware. Simple red-clay, lead-glazed pottery in pinkish buffs, reds and browns.

Reform Flasks. Spirit flasks of brown salt-glazed stoneware in the form of prominent politicians, made at the time of the Reform Bill.

'Regent China'. Made by Chamberlain's Worcester factory from 1811.

Registry Mark. Mark of the 'Registration of Designs' Office, comprising code letters and numerals. Found on English earthenware 1842–67 and 1868–83.

Relief. Raised ornamentation.

Repairer. His job was to assemble the porcelain clay impressions of the various parts of a figure in readiness for the modeller.

Reserved. That part of the surface of an article left plain for the application of decoration.

'Resist' Lustre. See PEASANT STYLE.

Rhenish Stoneware. 16th-century imported German salt-glazed stoneware, often found with silver trimmings.

Reform Flask   **Queen's Pattern**   **Rockingham vase**

Rhenish 'Tigerware'. Mottled brown variety of Rhenish stoneware.

Rhodian Ware. Rhodian is a misnomer for Isnik. See ISNIK POTTERY.

'Rice-grain' Decoration. Found on Persian pottery and Chinese porcelain. Small perforations filled with transparent glaze.

Ridgway Earthenware and Porcelain. The Ridgways were potters from the end of the 18th century. Notable among their pioneer achievements was the process of photographic reproduction as a form of decoration.

Rockingham. Bone china made by the Brameld brothers from 1820.

'Rockingham' Glaze. Lustrous purple-brown lead glaze, stained with manganese, made at Swinton in the early 19th century.

Rockingham (U.S.). Frequently, but incorrectly, called 'Beddington ware'. Manufactured in large quantities in numerous American factories from 1840 onwards. Yellow, with lustrous purple-brown lead glaze applied in mottled or streaked patterns.

Rockwood Faience. Emanated from Cincinnati, Ohio, in 1880. Consisted first of table wares, later extended to range of 'art' wares.

Rogin. Japanese lacquer-work technique, using powdered silver.

Roiro. Japanese. Highly polished black lacquer.

Rorstrand Pottery. Production of Swedish factory operating from 1726.

Rose du Barry. Incorrect description of coloured ground on Sèvres porcelain, properly called Rose Pompadour.

Rose Pompadour. See ROSE DU BARRY.

Rose-engine-turning. Basketwork patterns produced on porcelain and pottery by an engine-lathe.

Rosso Antico. Josiah Wedgwood's name for his red stoneware.

Rouen Faience. Tin-glazed earthenware made at Rouen from the 14th century.

Rouen Porcelain. Made at Rouen between 1673 and 1700.

Rouge de Fer. Iron-red enamel used on Chinese porcelain.

'Ruby-back' Decoration. Variety of *famille rose* porcelain. See FAMILLE ROSE.

'S' Mark. Associated with Caughley porcelain.

Sabeji. Japanese rust-coloured lacquer.

St Cloud Porcelain. Products of porcelain factory established near Versailles c. 1700.

Salopian Mark. Associated with the Caughley porcelain factory.

Salt Kit. Used for storing salt. Dome-topped ovoid jar surmounted by knob, with loop handle and circular opening at side.

Salt-glazed Stoneware. Produced by a process of throwing salt into the kiln when at maximum temperature.

Samson Porcelain Factory. Paris factory noted for reproductions of early Chinese armorial porcelain.

San T'sai (Three Colour) Ware. Commonly associated with Ming 3-colour ware, but also applicable to porcelains enamelled 'on the biscuit' in *famille verte* yellow, green and purple in K'ang Hsi period.

Sang-de-Boeuf. Range of ox-blood monochromes used on early Chinese porcelain.

St Cloud Porcelain figure

Salt-glazed Stoneware jug

Satsuma Ware. Pottery made on the Japanese island of Kyu shu from the early 17th century; exported in large quantity in the 19th century.

Savona Maiolica. Tin-glazed earthenware made at Savona, Italy, in the 17th and 18th centuries.

'Scale' Ground. Known also as 'fish-scale' pattern; particular to Worcester porcelain.

Sceaux Porcelain. Manufactured at Sceaux, Seine, from c. 1748 to 1794.

Schwartzlot. Black monochrome decoration, sometimes enhanced with iron-red or gold, first used by the Dutch glass decorators and the Nuremberg glass and faience painters, later for Du Paquier porcelain.

73

'Scratch Blue' Ware. White salt-glazed stoneware with incised floral or bird decorations, etc., made before firing stage.

'Scratch Brown' Ware. Salt-glazed stoneware with decorative incisions filled with brown pigment.

'Scratch Cross' Family. Porcelain wares with incised cross on inside of foot-ring.

Scroll Salt. 17th-century salt-cellar in Lambeth delftware.

'Secret' Decoration. See AN HUA.

Semi-china. Porcellanous earthenware.

'Scratch Blue' Ware   Sèvres Porcelain jar

Septre Mark. Associated with Berlin porcelain.

Sèvres Porcelain. Made at Vincennes from 1738. In the 1750s the factory was taken over by Louis XV. The wares were famous for their brilliant ground colours. See also: ROSE POMPADOUR, BLEU-DE-CIEL, OEIL-DE-PERDRIX, PÂTE-SUR-PÂTE.

'S & G' Mark. Found on Isleworth earthenware. The factory for the production of this ware was established about 1760 and closed about sixty years later; probably produced the zig-zag patterned 'Welsh' wares.

Sgraffito. Pottery decoration achieved by scratching through slip and revealing pattern of body colour.

'Shadowy Blue' Ware. See YING CH'ING WARE.

Shield Mark. Associated with Vienna and Nymphenburg porcelain.

'Shield Toby' Jug. So named for a shield found on left side with words: 'It's all out then fill him again.'

Shrinkage. Contraction of porcelain after firing.

Shu Fu ('Privy Council') Ware. Porcelain of the Chinese Yüan dynasty.

Sgraffito decoration. Shield mark. Vienna, 1850–64; Nymphenburg, 1800

Siamese Twins. Inspired by the Siamese twins, Eliza and Mary Chulkhurst, born about 1680 at Biddenden, Kent. Their birth was commemorated on a sgraffito dish and Bristol delft platter; the twins also appear on redware copies of the 'Biddenden' cake, an annual dole.

Siegburg Stoneware. Made near Bonn from the Middle Ages to 1632.

Slipware 'cradle' and typical designs

Slip. Liquid clay for making, coating or decorating pottery.

Slipware. Earthenware decorated with white or coloured slip (q.v.).

Smalt. Glass coloured blue with cobalt, the pigment being made by pulverising it. Used in the making of enamels for pottery and porcelain decoration.

'Smaltino'. Maiolica is the name given to tin-glazed earthenware made in Spain and Italy from the 14th century. Smaltino is contemporary name for this ware as it was made in Italy, especially in Venice, in the 16th century.

'Snowman' Figures. Produced in porcelain at Longton Hall.

Snufftaker. Toby jug representing old man taking snuff.

Soapstone. Steatite ingredient of English soft-paste porcelain paste.

Soft-paste Porcelain. Softer and less refractory than hard-paste porcelain; treated with lead glaze after which it is given a second firing at a lower temperature.

Somerset. Lead-glazed pottery made near Ilminster, at Donyatt (mid-17th century onwards) and at Crock Street (in 18th and 19th centuries); designs incised and glaze stained green in patches.

South Staffordshire Enamel. Snuff-boxes, wine labels, candlesticks, etc., produced in this area in the mid-18th century.

Southwark Delftware. So-called Lambeth delftware was also made at Southwark. See also LAMBETH DELFTWARE.

Spatter. Range of pottery made for the American market in Staffordshire c. 1820–50.

Spinario. Copy of boy figure extracting thorn from foot in the Capitoline Museum, Rome.

Spode. Factory founded in 1770. Early productions in earthenware. Later, established process for the manufacture of fine quality bone china, which was to provide the basic formula up to the present day.

'Sponged' Ware. Rough decorative effect achieved by sponging ware with pigment, and by free painting.

Spout-cup. Early 18th century; for feeding infants and invalids.

Sprigged Decoration. Application of relief ornament to pottery or porcelain from metal or hard-plaster mould.

Spur Marks. Marks left on porcelain or pottery from the spurs on which the wares are placed after glazing and during the firing process.

'Squire' Jug. Toby jug; representation of seated squire figure.

Staffordshire. Porcelain and pottery made in Staffordshire, the centre of the English pottery industry. The name is particularly applied to cottages, and figures of animals and people.

'Snowman' figure   Spode teapot   'Squire' Toby jug

Fox's mask Stirrup-cup

Stone China dish

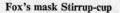

Star Mark. Associated with Doccia and Nove porcelain.

Statuary Porcelain. Original name of Parian ware (q.v.).

Steatite. See SOAPSTONE.

Steen. Earthen vessel for liquid; later used for bread, meat or fish.

'Step' Toby Jug. Representation of seated figure holding pipe; probably the first toby jug to be modelled.

Stirrup-cup. Made in earthenware and porcelain as well as in silver. Trophy cup often in form of fox's or greyhound's mask, without handles.

Stone China. Cheap substitute for porcelain; hard white earthenware containing china-stone.

Stoneware. Pottery made from very silicious clay or from composition of clay and flint.

Stork Mark. Associated with The Hague porcelain.

Stork mark

Sunderland Ware ewer   **Sussex Slipware jar**   **Swansea spill vase**

Strasbourg Faience. Product of Strasbourg factory founded in 1721.

Sunderland Ware. Mostly transfer-printed cream-coloured earthenware manufactured in the Sunderland area in the 18th and 19th centuries.

Sung Dynasty. Period 960 to 1279, noted for the excellence of its felspathic stoneware production and for the beauty of its pottery shapes and glazes.

Supper-set. Circular covered dish with receptacles for four open dishes; made of silver, plate or porcelain.

Sussex Pig. Pottery jug in form of pig with detachable head serving as cup, intended to hold a hogshead of liquor. 19th century.

Sussex Slipware. White inlay pattern and streaked glaze: two characteristic forms of decoration found on this ware, which was made in the late 18th and early 19th century.

Swansea Earthenware and Porcelain. The Cambrian Pottery at Swansea was founded in the 1760s. Among other things it was responsible for the production of a particular translucent duck-egg green paste.

T'ang Dynasty box

Temmoku bowl

'Swatow' Ware. Made in South China; thickly glazed and roughly finished, with powerful style of decoration. Late 16th to 17th century.

'T' and 'T°' Marks. Associated with Bow, Bristol and Plymouth porcelain.

Talavera Maiolica. Succeeded Hispano-Moresque maiolica (q.v.) at the end of the 16th century.

T'ang Dynasty. Period 618 to 906, the golden age of Chinese culture which, especially, marked the invention of translucent white porcelain.

Tao Kuang Period. Period 1821–50.

Tê-hua Porcelain. See BLANC-DE-CHINE.

Tea-canister. Container for tea in caddy made of glass, metal or earthenware. 18th century.

Temmoku. Japanese name for porcelain wares with lustrous brown glaze, notably Sung Chien wares.

Texts. Inscribed verses, decorated with clock, sun and moon, and set either in wall plaques with lustre 'frames' or in cottage mantelpiece ornaments.

'Thin Man' Toby Jug. Representation of thin man holding beer mug and pipe.

Thuringian Porcelain. See LIMBACH PORCELAIN.

Tickenhall. Derbyshire slipwares were made at Tickenhall, where pottery had been made from the middle ages. Tickenhall ware is usually associated with a dark brown earthenware,

Example of Text

'Tigerware' jug

decorated and shaped with added pads of soft clay; 17th century.

'Tigerware' Jug. Imported from Germany in the 16th century; big-bellied, salt-glazed pitcher, sometimes embellished with silver.

Tin Enamelled Earthenware. English imitation of Delftware (q.v.), made from mid-16th century.

Tin Glaze. Lead glaze to which tin ash has been added to render it opaque.

Ting. Chinese incense-burner in the form of a small three-footed cauldron.

Ting Ware. Porcelain of the Sung dynasty, and later. Sometimes decorated with flowers, fishes, etc., incised under the glaze.

Ting Ware plate

T° mark

81

Example of 'Tithe Pig'

'Tithe Pig'. Figure subject in porcelain or earthenware made prior to the abolition of the tithe system in 1836.

Toad Mugs. Common in the North Country in the 19th century. When the mug is drained the figure of a toad is found in the bottom.

Tobi Seiji. Japanese name for brown-spotted Sung celadon wares of LUNG-CHÜAN.

Toby Fillpot. Nickname of Harry Elwes, a celebrated toper, who served as the model for the original toby jug.

Toby Jug. Jug or mug usually in the form of a man with three-

Toad Mug

Toby Jug (sailor)

cornered hat, holding beer mug and pipe. Made in a number of character representations.

Togidashi. Japanese lacquer-work technique; literally 'polishing out' coloured design to completely smooth surface.

Tortoiseshell Ware. Lead-glazed cream earthenware stained to give tortoiseshell effect, made about the middle of the 18th century.

Tou Ts'ai Enamel. Literally, 'contrasting colour'. Juxtaposition on a variety of Chinese porcelain wares of delicate designs in underglaze blue with transparent enamel colours.

Tournai Porcelain. Made from the mid-18th century at Tournai in Belgium, in the manner of Sèvres, Chelsea and Worcester.

Tortoiseshell Ware plate

Trailed Slip decoration

Trailed Slip. Slip 'trailed' from a spouted vessel in the decoration of pottery.

'Transitional' Period. 17th century; between the Ming period of Wan Li and the K'ang Hsi revival. Blue-and-white and Ming 'five-colour' style wares were made in this period.

Translucent Enamel. Capable of transmitting light without being transparent.

Triangle marks

Triangle Mark. Associated with Chelsea porcelain.

Triple Reed Dish. Dish with number of mouldings on edge of rim.

Turquoise Blue Glaze. A brilliant glaze of the Ming '3-colour' class.

'Twyford' Toby Jug. Otherwise known as 'Step' toby jug (q.v.).

Tyg. 17th- and 18th-century mug with from two to twelve handles for drinking in the company of convivial spirits.

Tz'u Chou Ware. Stoneware made in this part of China from the Sung dynasty until the present day.

Unaker. China clay.

Underglaze Colours. Of the metallic oxides cobalt and manganese purple are among the very few than can stand up to the high temperature of glaze firing. Underglaze blue was frequently used for Chinese porcelain of the Ming period and the secret of its use was rediscovered in the manufacture of Meissen porcelain. Underglaze decoration is applied to the biscuit pottery before the addition of the glaze.

Tyg with four handles

Tz'u Chou Ware

Underglaze Decoration. Applied to porcelain or pottery biscuit before glazing process.

Urbino Maiolica. Made at Urbino and Castel Durante (q.v.) from the 16th century.

Urn. Two-handled vase with domed lid, of classical origin.

Usk Japanned Ware. Made by two of the Allgood brothers near Pontypool, Monmouthshire, from the 1760s.

Venice Porcelain. Made at two factories at Venice in the 18th century, one making hard-paste porcelain (see Vezzi porcelain), the other making the soft-paste variety.

Vicar and Moses

Vienna Porcelain figure

Venisons. Set of bowls fitting one into the other, c. 1800–50.

Vermicelli Ground. Patterned ground on porcelain resembling wriggling threads of vermicelli, usually in gold.

Vezzi Porcelain. Made by Francesco Vezzi, who started a hard-paste porcelain factory at Venice in 1720.

Vicar and Moses. Popular Staffordshire figure piece in the second half of the 18th century; depicts vicar asleep in the pulpit with parish clerk below, conducting the service.

Vienna Porcelain. Made at a factory founded in 1717 by Du Paquier, Hunger and Stoelzel (both the latter from Meissen; one an enameller, the other an arcanist).

Vincennes Porcelain

Vincennes Porcelain. Vincennes was the first location of the Sèvres porcelain factory.

Vinovo Porcelain. Made at Vinovo (Turin) between 1776 and 1820.

Volkstedt Porcelain. Thuringian factory making soft-paste and, later, hard-paste porcelain.

'W' Mark. Associated with Berlin and Wallendorf (Limbach) porcelain.

'W*' Mark.** Impressed mark of Enoch Wood, late 18th- and early 19th-century pottery manufacturer.

Wall Pocket. Staffordshire salt-glazed flower or spill vase in the shape of horn of plenty, fish, or mask.

Wallendorf Porcelain. Wallendorf was one of the Limbach factories, established in 1764.

Walton, John, Pottery Figures. Early 19th century; figures set against tree backgrounds and brightly enamelled.

Wall Pocket   **Wan Li Period bowl**   **Walton Pottery figure**

Wan Li Period. Many pieces were exported to Europe during this period (1573–1619).

Warburton. Late 18th-century makers of creamware, from Cobridge, Staffordshire.

Wassail Bowl. A variety of loving cup, deriving its name from ancient fertility rites.

Examples of Wedgwood

'Welsh' Ware dish

Wedgwood. Pottery made at Etruria, a village near Stoke-on-Trent, founded by Josiah Wedgwood (1730–95); especially fine porcelain with small cameo reliefs in white paste on a tinted matt ground.

Wednesbury. South Staffordshire enamelling trade centre from the last quarter of the 18th century.

Weesp Porcelain. Dutch hard-paste porcelain made from 1764.

'Welsh' Ware. Meat dishes in shape of gardener's trug (shallow basket made of wood strips).

'Welshman' Toby Jug. Representation of seated figure with goat between his knees.

Wheel Mark. Associated with Hoechst porcelain.

'Whieldon' Ware. Type of cream-coloured glazed earthenware made by Thomas Whieldon (1719–95) treated to give it a tortoiseshell or mottled effect.

White Porcelain. Chinese porcelain originating in the Tang dynasty and assuming a variety of decoration motifs through successive periods.

Willow Pattern. Popular porcelain pattern used by a number of factories; not a genuine Chinese motif.

Wincanton Pottery. Tin-glazed earthenware made at Wincanton in the second quarter of the 18th century.

Worcester Porcelain. Started in mid-18th century. A third Worcester factory was absorbed by Royal Worcester in 1889.

Typical Willow pattern   **Worcester cup and saucer**

'Wreathing'. Defect in thrown porcelain wares in form of spiral marks.

Wrotham Pottery. Mostly wares for domestic use made at Wrotham in the 17th and 18th centuries.

Wu Ts'ai Ware. Literally 'five-colour'. Wan Li period Chinese porcelain.

Yasuriko. Japanese lacquer-work technique involving the sprinkling of metal filings.

Yellow Ware. Utility ware moulds, baking dishes, etc., made of cream or buff clays and transparently glazed in a range of yellows. Rockingham ware has the addition of mottled brown manganese colouring. c. 1830–1900.

Yi-Hsing Stoneware. Introduced to Europe from China with the new fashion of tea drinking in the late 17th century. Early examples elegantly shaped; 19th-century versions tended to be crudely enamelled.

Ying Ch'ing Ware. Chinese porcelain with brilliant transparent 'shadowy blue' glaze, mostly from the Sung dynasty period.

York House. Painted enamels factory in Battersea in the mid-18th century.

Ying Ch'ing Ware
vase

Yi-Hsing Stoneware
teapot

Yüeh Ware
flask

Yorkshire. Trailed and marbled slipware introduced in the 18th century and manufactured at Howcans, Swill Hill, Burton-in-Lonsdale and Midhope.

Yüan Dynasty. Period of SHU FU porcelain 1279–1368.

Yüeh Ware. Chinese celadon ware from the 3rd to 11th century.

Yung Cheng Porcelain vase

Zurich Porcelain figure

Yung Cheng Porcelain. Period of particular elegance and refinement (1725–35), when *famille rose* began to supplant *famille verte* enamels.

'Z' Mark. Associated with Zürich porcelain.

Zaffer. Powdered cobalt oxide for the manufacture of smalt used for the colouring of pottery.

Zürich Porcelain. Made at a factory established in 1763. Notable for its figures.

PART TWO

Glass

Agata Glass. Made at Cambridge, Mass. Resembles peach-blow (q.v.), with a spattered mottling on a glossy finish.

Agate Glass. Of variegated colours to resemble agate. Popular during the Renaissance.

Air-twist Stem. Frequently found on 18th-century drinking glass. Spiral inset in drawn stem, executed in a variety of forms by the extension of air bubbles. Also called Wormed Stem.

Ale Glass. Distinguished by long and relatively narrow bowl, sometimes with lipped rim and engraved with motif of hops and barley. From the 18th century.

Amberina Glass. Made by the New England Glass Company. Lead glass, usually blown with lustrous finish of pale amber shading to ruby.

Amelung Glassworks. Named after John Frederik Amelung, who left Germany for America in the late 18th century.

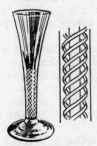

Air-twist Stem

Ale Glass

American Glass dish. Anglo-Venetian Glass. Arch and Sprig motif

Products include flint table glass, decanters, looking glass for mirrors, etc.

American Flint Glassworks. Mid-19th-century works in Boston, Mass., which produced a wide variety of pressed and cut glass ware.

American Glass. Glass making was one of the first crafts established by the American colonists in the 17th century. Earliest examples are greenish in colour, coarse in texture, and full of bubbles.

Anglo-Venetian Glass. Fine soda-glass vessels made in London in the 16th and 17th centuries in the Venetian manner.

Angular Knop. Protuberance on stem of glass.

Annealing. Processing in hot ovens to strengthen glass prior to cutting designs on it.

Annulated Knop. Flattened protuberance on stem of glass accompanied by two, four or six knops of graduating size.

Arch and Sprig. Repetitive motif encircling sweetmeat bowls.

Baccarat Glassworks. Famous in 19th-century France as specialists in the making of glass for optical purposes, and millefiore and other paperweights. Work of father and son Battestini. Still in operation.

Bakewell, Pears & Co. Glassworks founded in America by

two Englishmen in 1802, known for production of decanters, bottles, flasks, vases, drinking glasses, candelabra, etc.

Bakhmeteff. Russian glassworks founded in the 18th century; operated until the 1917 revolution.

Ball Knop. Large spherical knop often found immediately above a silesian stem. See also KNOP and SILESIAN STEM.

Baltimore Glassworks. Founded towards the end of the 18th century. Production: bottles and flasks in various colours.

Baluster. Term for glass stems having outline similar to balusters of wood. Earlier edition known also as the Portuguese swell. Purpose of design, to ensure safety in lifting glass.

Baccarat paperweight.   **Baluster Stems.**   **Example of Beaker**

Batch. Term indicating a mixture of raw materials prepared for melting.

Beaker. 16th-century predecessor of the tumbler. Sometimes known as 'bellying goblet', for drinking cider.

Bell Bowl. Deep-waisted bowl with wide mouth and incurved profile. Also called Bell Glass.

Bevelled Glass. Mirror-plate with angled edges.

Bladed Knop. See KNOP, of which there are many varieties. A bladed knop is a thin, sharp-edged, flattened knop placed horizontally on the stem.

Blobs. Small lumps of molten glass applied to blown glass as decoration.

Bloom. Opaque film sometimes found covering the surface of English and more often Irish flint glass.

Blown-moulded Glass. See MOULD-BLOWN GLASS.

Bohemian Glass tankard

Blowpipe. Long, hollow iron tube used for blowing glass.

Blue Glass. Manufactured at Bristol and other glassmaking centres, where the blue tint was obtained by the addition of cobalt. Popular in the 18th century.

Blue Tint. Faint blue tint applied to some late Georgian flint-glass; examples from Waterford, Derby, Stourbridge, Bristol, and elsewhere.

Bohemian Glass. Thought to have originated in Venice. From the 16th century onwards was made in Bohemia, the centre of the crystal glass making industry. Found in various shades of red, blue, amber and green; noted for its engraving and the cutting through of an opaque coloured outer surface to reveal clear or ground glass pattern beneath.

Booze Bottles. Name applied to bottles intended for whisky,

Bristol Glass

Bucket Form Bowl

especially those produced in 1860 by the Whitney Glass Works for Edmund G. Booz of Philadelphia.

Bottle Glass. Greenish or brownish tone produced by impurity in the silica employed in glass manufacture.

Bristol Glass. In the 17th and early 18th century the Bristol glasshouses were mainly engaged in making window glass or bottles. Later a variety of small glass wares were made in deep blue, purple or green. Ornamental vases, candlesticks, etc., were made at the same time in an opaque white glass annealed to a point of unprecedented toughness.

Broad Glass. Flat sheet glass.

Broad Street Glasshouse. Established in London in the 16th century by Giacomo Verzelini (see Part 7) for the making of Venetian-style glass.

Bucket Form Bowl. 18th- and 19th-century form of drinking glass bowl in form of a bucket.

Bull's Eye. American term for medium-sized to small round mirror with ornate frame, fashionable in the early 19th century.

Bullett Knop. Small spherical protuberance on stem of drinking glass. See KNOP.

Cameo Glass replica of the Portland Vase

Cameo Glass. Plain-coloured glass with partial or complete coating of opaque white glass upon which a relief ornament is carved.

Canes. Slender cylinders of enamel used in the decoration of glassware, notably paperweights.

Carriage Glass. Stemless drinking glass for serving travellers or riders.

Case Bottles. Four-sided bottles made to fit compartments of cases or boxes.

Cased Glass. Different coloured glass laid over clear glass to produce patterned effect. 19th-century Bohemian technique.

Cased Glass vase

Type of Champagne Glass

Champagne Glass. Has taken several forms since the introduction of the wine into England in the 17th century: the flute glass, the expansive bowl on a slender stem of the 19th century and onwards, and the tulip-shaped glass introduced about the middle of the 19th century.

Clichy Paperweights. Identified by symbol of pink and white rose in the pattern; also a purple rose or open purple flower. Signed C. or, in rare cases, CLICHY. The 19th-century Clichy glasshouse, near Paris, also provided optical glass.

Coaching Glass. 19th-century drinking cup, intended to be emptied at one draught.

Coaching Glass   Clichy paperweight   Coin Glass

Coin Glasses. Glasses containing a coin in the knop in the stem.

Collar Knop. Collar of glass at one or other or both ends of stem of glass.

Colour-twist Stem. Variant of the opaque white twist executed in single and sometimes two or three colours—mostly blue, green and red. 18th-century.

Coloured Glass. Generic term covering a variety of glass ware, tinted by the addition of natural or prepared metallic oxides (e.g. BOHEMIAN GLASS)

Compound-twist Stem. Stem having single air column spiral down its centre enclosed in multiple opaque white twist.

Cordial Glass. Glass with small bowl on tall, stout stem introduced in the 17th century. More delicate designs were executed in the 18th century, with air-twist, opaque-twist and facet-cut stems, and with engraved bowls.

Cords. Slight striae (undulating markings) which can be felt with the fingers on the surface of the glass.

Typical Cordial Glasses

Crisselled Glass dish

Cork Glasshouse decanter

Cork Glasshouse. Established in Ireland in 1783. Noted for clarity and brilliance of its flint-glass and for its hand-cut work.

Cork Terrace Glasshouse. Established in Ireland in 1819. Specialists in cut and engraved dessert services.

Costrel. Pilgrim's bottle, designed to be suspended from a cord or sling.

Crackled Glass. Effect thought to have been attained by the sudden cooling of the surface when the object was half blown. Probably first practised by the Venetians in the 16th century.

Crisselled Glass. Or crizzled glass. Defect in glass caused by

Example of Cut Glass **Domed Foot** **Diamond-point Engraving**

imbalance of ingredients, manifested in clouding of the material.

Crown Glass. Flat glass so blown as to leave a bull's eye in the middle.

Crystal. Term used in glassmaking to denote the finest clear flint glass.

Cullet. Broken flint glass added to the batch (q.v.).

Cup Bowl. See BUCKET-FORM BOWL, of which the Cup-bowl is a less common form. Sometimes coloured green.

Cusp. A centrally placed stem knop shaped by cutting.

Cut Glass. The glass has to be well annealed to make it strong enough to accept all-over cutting. Introduced in the early 18th century.

Cyst. A rounded protuberance in the base of a wine bowl.

D'Alva Bottles. Ale-house bottles, named after Fernando Alvarez de Toledo, Duke of Alva (1508–83).

Diamond-point Engraving. Pattern inscribed by hand on glass with the point of a diamond.

Domed Foot. Foot of vessel of glass or silver in shape of flat or terraced dome.

Typical Dram Glasses

Enamel-twist glass

Dram Glasses. Also known as nips, joeys, ginettes, and gin glasses. Made in a variety of forms, all of a rather rudimentary order, since the 17th century.

Drawn Stem. Drawn from a gathering of metal at the base of the bowl; plain knopped or baluster stem.

Drop Knop. Knop resembling frustum of inverted cone, half an inch to an inch above the foot.

Dwarf Ale Glass. Version of ale glass with or without short or absent stem. 18th century.

Enamel-twist. Enamel threads in spiral shapes incorporated in stems of drinking glasses.

Enamelled Glass. Ancient technique which takes several forms including opaque-whites and various colourings.

Engraved Glass. Technique for engraving glass calls for the application of emery powder, mixed with oil, to the edges of small revolving discs.

Etched Glass. Designs of singular delicacy are achieved by etching on glass first coated with wax.

Facet. Small surface of glass, or other ground material, cut at an angle to other, similar surfaces.

Facet-cut Stem. Stem of drinking glass cut with facets in diamond or hexagonal shape. Popular design in the second half of the 18th century.

Example of Facet

Facet-cut Stem

Façon D'Altare. In the manner of the craftsmen at the glass-works at Altare, near Genoa, founded originally by emigrants from Normandy.

Façon de Venise. In the manner of the Venetian craftsmen at Murano, near Venice.

Finger Bowls. Known as wash-hand glasses, finger cups, finger glasses. From c. 1760.

Fire-polishing. Re-heating finished glassware at furnace to remove tool or other marks caused in manufacture.

Firing Glasses. Stumpy drinking glasses with thick, heavy feet and small capacity bowls. Often employed in the 18th century to rap table in response to a toast.

Flasks. Flat, oval bottles carried when travelling. Scent flasks are smaller and made in a variety of shapes.

Finger Bowl

Firing Glass

Folded Foot

Example of Flint Glass   **Flute Glass**

Flat Cutting. See PANEL CUTTING.

Flint Glass. Normally used for press work until the 1860s when a glass prepared with soda and lime as a flux was found to be less costly. Also known as lead crystal.

Flowered Glasses. Georgian cordial or ratafia glasses, sometimes called surfeit glasses since the narrow bowl (often engraved with flowers) minimised the evaporation of the surfeit water.

Flute Glass. Light-weight soda glass dating from time of Charles I, or even earlier, with long conical bowls and attached to the foot by a short decorative knop.

Folded Foot. A foot reinforced by folding it over on itself thus forming a narrow hollow rim on the upper surface. This form later developed into a flat welt folded beneath the rim. Also called Welted foot.

Foot. Base of glass, the shape of which is a frequent aid in the determination of the glass's period.

Free Blown Glass. Blown and manipulated with hand tools and without the aid of moulds.

Frigger. Colloquial term for experimental or apprentice

piece of glass, and for such knick-knacks as glass walking-sticks, bells, tobacco pipes, etc.

Funnel Bowl. As its name suggests, a bowl which is narrow at the base and increases in diameter to the edge.

Gather. A blob of molten metal secured at the end of a glass-blower's blowpipe prior to blowing.

Georgian Ale. Georgian wine glass with long bowl, capacity 4–5 ozs.

Georgian Dram. Small version of Georgian wine glass, capacity up to 2 ozs.

Giant Ale. 18th-century glass over 12″ in height.

Gimmal Flask. Flask or bottle, mostly used to contain oil or vinegar, with separate compartments, each with a spout.

Gin Glass. See DRAM GLASSES.

Ginette. See DRAM GLASSES.

Glass Bottle Seals. Late 17th-century seals marking quart size wine bottles, impressed with owner's crest or cypher or, were owner a vintner, with badge, initials or tavern sign.

Glass Overlays. 'Cups' specially blown to fit over piece after it has been made.

Glass Pictures. Descriptive of back-painting, under-glass painting, mirror painting, gold-glass engraving, *verre églomisé*, glass silhouettes, etc.

Glass Silhouettes. Silhouettes painted on to glass by various processes, such as gold-glass engraving, *verre églomisé*, etc.

Glass Walking- Stick. See also FRIGGER. Mostly made in the

Glass Bottle Seals

Typical Goblet

late 18th-century Nailsea glasshouse. The majority are enriched with coloured spiral threads.

Goblet. Drinking glass with bowl disproportionately large in relation to the height of the stem. Capacity, a gill or more.

Green Glass. Coloured glass produced in Bristol and London in the mid-18th century; also imported from Bohemia. Green paperweights made at Bristol and Nailsea, 1818. Softer greens in flint glass examples date from c. 1845.

'Greene' Glasses. Drinking glasses sold in the 17th century by the firm of John Greene and Michael Measey, made by Morelli of Venice. Drawings of these glasses survive and may be seen in the British Museum.

Hand Blown Glass. See FREE BLOWN GLASS.

Herring-bone Fringe or Blaze. Delicately cut parallel mitres vertical or slanting, encircling early 19th-century glasses.

Hollow Cutting. Method of decorating glasses by cutting shallow concavities. Form of 'hollow diamonds' much used in the mid-18th century.

Hollow Stems. Represented a brief vogue in the mid-18th and mid-19th centuries. The intention was that the sediment from the wine should sink down the stem leaving the liquid in the bowl clear.

GLASS

'Greene' Glasses

Example of Incised Stem

Hollow-ware. Generic term for vessels made to contain liquid.

Hollowed. Punty scar worn smooth. See PUNTY.

Ice Glass. From the 16th-century Venetian method of decorating glass; cracked ice effect achieved by plunging hot glass in water and later reheating it.

Incised Stem. One of many stem designs; made by tooling the plastic glass with vertical ribs and immediately twisting the stem.

Insufflated. Term used to describe early glass hitherto known as 'contact three section blown mould'.

Jacobite Glasses. Glasses bearing propaganda in form of emblems and mottoes; a six petalled rose with one or two buds was a commonly used emblem.

Jelly Glass. Tall, gracefully waisted dessert glass with one or two looped handles, much used in the 18th century.

Jacobite Glass

Jelly Glass

105

Example of a Kick

Kit-Cat Glass

Joey. See DRAM GLASS.

Kick. Dent in form of pyramid found in base of many pre-1760 decanters, bowls and bottles.

Kit-Cat Glass. Baluster wine glass called after the 18th-century Kit-Cat Club.

Knop. Flattened spherical or polygonal bulb or protuberance on stem of glass.

Lace Glass. See VITRO DI TRINA.

Lacy Glass. American term for glass with radiant appearance produced by adding tiny hemispheres of crystal to a pressed plate; c. 1818–40.

Latticino. Decoration or filigree. Introduced in Venice in the second quarter of the 16th century. A criss-cross mesh network of fine threads of coloured glass in spiral and numerous other designs.

Lead Glass. Glass containing lead oxide, introduced into

Knops: Angular, Annulated, Blended, Bullet, Drop, Mushroom

glassmaking c. 1675. The effect of lead is to make the glass softer and more malleable.

Lehr. Heated chamber or tunnel in which the glass is strengthened by annealing.

Lime Glass. Substitute for lead flint glass discovered in 1864 by William Leighton in West Virginia.

Loopings or Draggings. Decorative device used since ancient times in which the surface of the object is festooned with loops of coloured glass.

Mercury Twist Stem.   Example of Merese.   Milk Glass vase

Mercury Twist Stem. Air twists in large diameter spirals and close coils down the stem of a glass. 1745–65.

Merese. Sharp-edged, flattened glass button connecting bowl and stem, or between foot and stem of wine glass.

Metal. The substance of glass, either molten or in the finished form.

Mexican Glass. Made for 200 years after the Spanish Conquest; some beautifully incised and painted in gold.

Milk Glass. Or opaque glass. Produced by the addition of tin oxide, arsenic or the ashes of calcined bones. Bears a resemblance to porcelain.

107

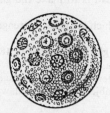 

Millefiore Glass.   Multiple Knops.   Moulded Pedestal Stem

Millefiore Glass. Technique derived from the Romans and applied particularly in France in the late 1840s in the enclosed decoration of paperweights and door stoppers. Innumerable patterns in circles, spirals, wheels, etc., in brilliant colours; also birds, butterflies, geometrical patterns, etc.

Mitre Cutting. Designs cut in glass with sharp-edged cutting wheel.

Mixed Twist Stem. Combination of air twist and opaque-white twist in single spiral down the stem. Late 1740s.

Monteith. A bowl, filled with water, used for cooling wine glasses. Also Monteigh.

Monteith. Or Bonnet glass. Punch or cheap sweetmeat glass introduced during reign of Charles II.

Mould-blown Glass. Glass made by blowing a gather of metal into a mould. From 1835 blow-moulded glass was finished by fire polishing.

Moulded Glass. Glass given its pattern and partial, or final, body shape by the mould into which it has been blown.

Moulded Pedestal Stem. Shouldered stem found on drinking glasses of the first half of the 18th century; also on candlesticks, sweetmeats and dessert-salvers of the second half of the 18th century.

Multiple Knops. Simple shaped knops repeated on stem.

108

Murano. Island near Venice famous for centuries for glass-making.

Mushroom Knop. Mushroom shaped protuberance found on stems of glasses with incurved or funnel bowls.

Nailsea Glass. Wide range of colourful trinkets and curios, also bottles, made at the Nailsea glasshouse, founded by John Lucas in 1788. The glass is brownish-green speckled with white.

Nevers Glass. See VERRE DE NEVERS.

New England Glass Company. Founded in 1818 at Cambridge, Mass., by Edward H. Munroe.

New Jersey Glass. Made in various places in southern New Jersey in the late 18th and 19th centuries.

Nip. See DRAM GLASS.

'Nipt Diamond Wais'. Diamond-shaped network made by pinching together vertical threads or ribs of glass.

Noggin. Small drinking vessel. A noggin-bottle usually holds a ¼ pint.

Offhand Glass. Useful and ornamental articles made by early American glassmakers from leftover ends of batches designed as gifts for friends.

Examples of Nailsea Glass   **'Nipt Diamond Wais'**

Ogee Bowls: single (*above*), double (*below*). **'Opal' Glass vase.**
Ovoid Bowl. Typical Passglas

Ogee Bowl. Bowl made in the shape of a double curve, the lower concave the upper convex, found on mid to late 18th-century drinking glasses. Double and triple ogee bowls were also made.

'Opal' Glass. Dating from early 19th century. Glass rendered semi-opaque by the addition of calcined bones.

Opaline. See 'OPAL' GLASS.

Opaque Glass. See MILK GLASS.

Opaque Twist Stems. Stems containing densely textured white enamel spirals, single or multiple, in fine hairs or broad tapes.

Ovoid Bowl. Found on many short ales and goblets.

Panel Cutting. Also known as flat cutting. Achieved by cutting pattern on flat end of grinding wheel. 18th century.

Paperweights. See Part 4.

Parison. Glassblower's term for an inflated, unformed gather of metal.

Passglas. German glass beaker with spiral threads round it so that when it is passed from guest to guest each has a proper measure.

Pâte-de-Verre. French process derived from the ancient

Egyptians. Glass of various colours is powdered and mixed and re-fired, after which it is moulded into the article required.

Pattern Glass. Name given to pressed glass produced in America since 1840.

Peachblow Glass. Name derived from Chinese peachblow porcelain; applied to glass made by a number of American factories, including the New England Glass Co. of Cambridge.

Phials. Small, narrow bottles used from the earliest times for unguents and medicines.

Pinched Trailing. Applied bands of glass pinched into a wavy formation.

Pomona Glass. Made by the New England Glass Co. A variety of clear glass etched and stained after being blown in a part-sized mould and then expanded.

Pontil. See PUNTY.

Potash Glass. Glass fluxed with unrefined vegetable ashes.

Potemkin. Prince Gregoire, owner of the Manufacture Imperiale de Cristal, founded in 1777. Revived by Alexander I in 1804, this factory continued to turn out fine glass until the end of the 19th century.

Potichomanie. Type of decoration on glass vases, in imitation of porcelain or pottery, fashionable in the middle of the 19th century.

Pressed Glass. Glass shaped mechanically in moulds.

Pinched Trailing

Prismatic Cutting

Purled Ornament

Raven's Head Seal

Prismatic Cutting. Sometimes known as step cutting. A method of cutting glass vessels in deep relief in a pattern of horizontal prisms on a curved surface.

Prunt. Glass seal or blob, plain or tooled, or moulded into a variety of shapes, applied to stem or bowl of drinking glass.

Punty. Or Pontil. Long iron rod attached to one end of blown glass after removal from the blowpipe. Punty or pontil mark is the scar left on blown glass when the punty is broken off.

Purled Ornament. All-over diaper moulding on glass vessels, having small round or oval compartments.

Quatrefoil Knop. A short knop pressed into four upright or twisted wings. Also called Wing Knop.

Quilling. American term; also known as 'pinched trailing'. Ornamentation employing coloured canes of glass in vertical stripes twisted into curved patterns.

Raven's Head Seal. Mark of George Ravenscroft (see Part 7) found on lead oxide or flint glass from 1675 onwards.

Reticulated. Also called 'expanded diamond', being a moulded pattern in the shape of a diamond.

Rib or Diamond Moulding. Diamond patterns on bowl of glass vessel formed by impressed straight or twisted lines.

Rib-twist Stem. See INCISED STEM.

Ricketts Glassworks. Bristol works notable for the production of bottles and cut glass throughout the 19th century. The first

Glass Rolling Pin

Typical Roemer

company to install the Donaldson furnace to improve the clarity of crystal glass.

Rigaree Trail. A process of applying vertical ribs of glass to a vessel while producing a more or less smooth surface.

Roemer. Drinking glass of a pale green colour, of medieval German origin which later became the traditional Rhenish wine glass. The stem is hollow and studded with prunts; the foot is hollow and conical.

Rolling Pins. Made by Nailsea and Bristol glassworks. Decorative containers in shape of rolling pins for holding salt.

Round Glass House. First flint glasshouse to be established in Ireland, in the 1690s.

Rummer. Short-stemmed drinking glass, used particularly for hot toddy. From the mid-18th century.

Example of a Rummer

'S' Reversed Mark. Associated with St Louis glasshouse.

St Louis Glassworks. Founded in France in the second half of the 18th century; noted for the production of millefiore paperweights.

Sandwich Glass. Made by Boston & Sandwich Glass Company at Sandwich, Mass., from 1825 to 1888.

Saratoga Glass. Produce of a New York factory established in 1844; delicately formed in light and dark green, amber and aquamarine coloured glass.

Scalloping. Rim outline formed by series of semi-circles.

Schmelzglas. See AGATE GLASS.

St Louis Glassworks paperweight

Sealed Glasses. The practice initiated by George Ravenscroft (see Part 7) of marking vessels with a seal was adopted by a number of other glassmakers up to the 1680s.

Seeds. Minute air bubbles caused by an insufficient furnace heat.

Short Ale Glasses. Like ale glasses but with shorter stems.

Short Cordial. Also known as 'Semi-cordial'. Like a cordial glass but with shorter stem.

Shouldered Stem. See MOULDED PEDESTAL STEM.

'Silesian' Stem. See MOULDED PEDESTAL STEM.

Silvered Glass. Made by the New England Glass Co. from the middle of the 19th century. A thin glass object was blown, then coated with a silvery substance, after which it was 'cupped' with another surface of glass.

Single-twist Stem. Found on drinking glasses of the second half of the 18th century. Consists of air, enamel or coloured thread spiral.

'S L' Mark. Mark of the first dated paperweights, made at the St Louis glassworks, France, in 1845.

Snuff Bottles. The Chinese made snuff bottles from glass or crystal as well as from jade, porcelain and rock crystal. Attached to the stopper was a tiny spoon for removing the snuff.

Soda Glass. Glass in which the principle flux is carbonate of lime.

Soda Glass

Step. Flattened button connecting stem of a rummer (q.v.) with its foot.

Stepped Lid. According to the elevations on the lid of a vessel, it might be single-stepped or double-stepped.

Stiegel Type Glassware. American factory in production from the 1760s; notable for tumblers engraved in the German manner and much coloured glass moulded with network.

Stones. Red and black specks found in early flint glass, the result of imperfect fusion between oxide of lead and silica.

Straight Funnel Bowl. Straight-sided bowl shaped like frustum of inverted cone.

Strawshank. See DRAWN STEM.

Sweetmeat Glass. Terraced Foot. A Tear in a wine glass

Striae. Undulations sometimes apparent in glass caused by working it before it has been properly molten.

Stuck Shank. Stem made from separate gather and welded to the base of the bowl.

Sulphides. Earliest glass paperweights, made in France and England. Contained white china plaque with relief modelling, embedded in glass.

Sweetmeat Glass. Sometimes referred to as 'dessert glasses' in the 18th century. See also JELLY GLASS.

Swelling Knop. Slight protuberance in the stem of a drinking glass containing an air tear.

Swirl Paperweight. Name given to paperweights containing spirals of coloured canes.

Tabernacle Mirror. American term for late 18th-century mirror with flat cornice, below which is a row of gilt balls above a scene painted on glass. The mirror is flanked by columns.

Tale-glass. Second-quality (glass) metal taken from the top of the pot.

Tears. Bubbles of air enclosed in stems or finials of drinking vessels as form of decoration.

Thistle Bowl

Three-piece Glass

Terraced Foot. Foot tooled in concentric circles.

Thistle Bowl. Bowl of drinking glass in thistle form: the bottom part is a solid or hollow sphere.

Thread Circuit. Thin trail of glass used as decoration round rim or neck of vessel.

Three-piece Glasses. Glasses the stems, bowls and feet of which have been separately made and moulded together.

Tint. Residual colour tinge in glass inherent in the ingredients of which the metal is composed.

Toasting Glass. Drinking glass with tall stem. The early toasting glass had a stem drawn from the bowl no thicker than one-eighth of an inch.

Toastmaster's Glass. In appearance the same as an ordinary drinking glass except that the bowl was solid with merely a

Toasting Glass

Toastmaster's Glass

GLASS

Toddy-lifter   **Example of Trumpet Bowl**   **Venetian Glass**

narrow v-shaped depression holding only half an ounce of liquor.

Toddy-lifter. Decanter-shaped pipette used to lift hot toddy from bowl to drinking glass.

Trailed Ornament. Technique by which looped threads of glass are applied to the surface of a glass vessel and melted in.

Trailing, Pinched. Applied threads of glass melted into the body of a vessel and pinched into a wavy pattern.

Trumpet Bowl. Waisted bowl of incurving shape merging into a drawn stem.

Tumbler Cup. Small plain drinking vessel round at the base and straight at the sides.

Two-piece Glasses. Drinking glasses in which the stem is drawn from the bowl and the foot is added.

Vauxhall Glasshouse. Established in the 1660s for the production of mirror glass.

Venetian Glass. Made on the island of Murano. Celebrated in the 15th, 16th and 17th centuries. Mainly thinly blown soda glass, worked at a low temperature.

Vermicular Collar. Wavy trail of glass round stem of glass vessel or round neck of decanter.

Verre de Fougère. French glass made from potash obtained from burning bracken.

Verre de Nevers. Glass from the French factory established at Nevers in the 16th century; notably small figures and 'toys'.

Verre Églomisé. A method of engraving in gold under glass named after Jean-Baptiste Glomy, a Parisian art dealer (died 1786).

Vertical Flute Cutting. From 1780 to 1790 stems were fluted above and below a central diamond-cut knop. In the following decade straight flutes were made from foot to bowl, knotched, horizontally grooved, or sliced.

Violin Bottles. American name mainly for whisky bottles, produced in a wide range of colours and sizes in the mid-19th century at glassworks in the Ohio River District.

Vitro di Trina

Waisted Bowl

Vitro di Trina. Also known as lace glass of Roman origin, carried forward by the 16th-century Venetians. Glass intricately patterned with threads of white glass within the clear glass.

Waisted Bowl. A variety of waisted bowls were popular in the latter part of the 18th century. The name suggests the shape of the reducing profile.

Waldglas. German version of VERRE DE FOUGÈRE.

Waterford decanter

Wine-glass Cooler

Waterford Glass. The celebrated Irish Waterford glasshouse was founded in 1784. Much of the deep cut glassware made at Waterford was exported to England.

Waterford (New Jersey) Glassworks. Established in the first quarter of the 19th century; makers of window glass, bottles and flasks.

Waterloo Glasshouse Company. Established at Cork in 1815; specialised in cut-glass table services for army messes.

Welted Foot. See FOLDED FOOT.

Wheel Engraving. Pattern cut by applying surface of glass to rapidly revolving wheel. English wheel engraved glass vessels date from the first quarter of the 18th century.

Old Wine Bottles

120

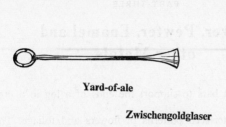

Yard-of-ale

Zwischengoldglaser

White Glassworks. Operated at Zanesville, Ohio, from 1815 to 1851.

Wine Bottles. Tin enamelled globular bottles from the 17th century, bearing initials, date and name of wine.

Wine-glass Coolers. Date from the middle of the 18th century to the 1860s. Similar to finger bowls with the exception of one or two lips in the rim. Also known as Monteiths or Monteighs (q.v.).

Wing Knop. See QUATREFOIL KNOP.

Wormed Stem. See AIR TWIST STEM.

Wrythening. Twisted or swirled ribbing or fluting on bowl or stem of drinking vessel.

Yard-of-ale. So called because it measured an ell—i.e. 1¼ yards. From late 17th century; underwent numerous changes in form throughout the 18th and 19th centuries.

Zwischengoldglaser. 18th-century German glass decorated with gold leaf, having as an accompaniment a second glass which fitted over it to protect the gilding.

PART THREE

Silver, Pewter, Enamel and other Metals

Andirons. Iron bars to support the ends of a log in a fire; fire-dogs.

Arabesque. Interlaced patterns of flowers and foliage. The motif is often found in combination with strapwork in the 16th century, and pierced work in the 18th century.

Argyle. Gravy container, shaped somewhat like a small coffee-pot, with an outer lining or inner container for hot water. In use about 1770 to 1800.

Asparagus Tongs. Asparagus server, derived from fish-slice, with spring-hinged upper jaw. Introduced in the last decade of the 18th century and subject to changes in design through the 19th century.

Assay-groove. Wriggled groove, up to the late 17th century, usually found close to the hall-marks. Means by which metal was taken for the purpose of assay (i.e. trial).

Bale Handle. Hooped or semi-circular handle, hinged on

Argyle

Basket for fruit, etc.

pivots or looped ears on hollow-ware (e.g. baskets, cream pails).

Basket. Used for bread, cake, fruit, also for dessert. Early circular examples succeeded by oval shapes with pierced bodies and swing handles, c. 1730. Later popular versions had wirework bodies with applied foliage, wheat and flowers, c. 1770. These were followed by solid bodies with engraved decoration.

Basting Spoon. Long handled, similar in shape to early punch-ladles. Probably for domestic use.

Battersea Enamel plaque

Beaker

Bat's-wing Fluting. External shaping to hollow-ware in form of graduated gadrooning curved to resemble shape of bat's wing.

Battersea Enamel. Produced at York House, Battersea, under Stephen Theodore Janssen (1753–6).

Beaker. Drinking vessel, usually tapered, without handles. Customarily plain, but early silver examples engraved or embossed.

Beefeater Flagon. Pewter flagon with lid resembling head-dress of the Yeomen of the Tower of London.

Beefsteak-dish. Similar to entrée dish. In a late 18th-century catalogue of Sheffield plate, John Cadman described it as being fitted with a 'handle to screw off to make a pair of dishes occasionally'.

123

Bell Horse Brass. Swinging bell to be found on the brasses on a martingale, or in a set above the horse's collar. 18th and 19th century.

Bells. Frequently formed centrepiece of inkstands up to mid-18th century, when usually fitted with baluster handles. Later, wood and ivory handles were used. Exceptional before 18th century.

Biggin. Silver coffee-pot with short spout, often mounted on stand with spirit-lamp.

Bell Horse Brasses

'Billies and Charlies'. Range of fake lead medallions and amulets made in London about the end of the 19th century. The name is a reference to their inventors.

Bilston. Early south Staffordshire centre of the enamelling trade. Produced large number of fine painted enamels notably, between 1740 and 1750, japanned snuff-boxes with enamel decoration.

Blackjack. 17th and 18th-century leader tankards occasionally mounted with silver rims.

Bleeding Bowl. See CUPPING BOWL.

Blowhole. Air vent in hollow castings or seamed hollow members; an escape device for air expanded by heat when soldering handles, finials and other such additions to the main body.

Bonbonnière. Small shaped sweetmeat boxes many of which were enamel painted to represent birds and birds' heads; also animals, fruit, etc.

Booge. Term used in the manufacture of pewter denoting the curved portion of a plate joining rim and bottom.

Book Hinges. Lid hinges of coffee-pots, jugs, etc., shaped like a book spine and having their pin joints capped with ornamental silver.

'Billies and Charlies'

Bottle Tickets. Silver (also Battersea enamel) discs, engraved with name of drink and suspended round neck of decanter by a chain. The engraver Simon-François Ravenet was responsible for a series, transfer-printed at Battersea, depicting 'boys' engaged in the task of producing the liquor relevant to the label.

Box Inkstand. Rectangular inkstand, made of silver, pewter or brass with one or two wells and drawers below.

Brandy-bowl. Flat, two-handled silver bowl for serving hot brandy; of 17th-century Scandinavian origin.

Bratina. A form of loving-cup, largely of Russian origin. Some were richly enamelled and decorated with gems.

Brazier. Precursor of the spirit-lamp stand, dating from the late 17th century. Circular bowl with pierced base plate for burning charcoal to heat kettles and dishes.

Brescian Steel. See CHISELLED AND CUT STEEL.

Bright-cut Engraving. Engraving by bevelled cutting on silverware and plate, popular in late 18th century.

Britannia Standard. In force 1697–1720; the Higher Standard for wrought silver plate [11 oz. 10 dwts. fine silver in the Pound Troy (12 oz.)]. The mark of Britannia replaced the sterling lion passant.

Bronze. Alloy of copper and tin, traditionally popular for its ease of working and the fine patina it acquires with age.

Bronze Disease. Corrosive incrustation formed on bronzes buried in the soil.

Bulbous Salt. Spherical salt-cellar, with shallow circular depression.

Butter-dish. Dating from the second half of the 18th century and usually associated with Ireland; oval pierced bowl and cover with glass liner. Later English examples were often circular tub-shaped.

C-scroll. Handle in form of letter 'C'. Also known as 'single scroll'.

Cake Basket. See BASKET.

Campana Vase. Early 19th century, bell-shaped, neo-classical style vase.

Cann. American term applied to a silver drinking vessel on a moulded base.

Cannel. Found near Wigan, Lancashire, and described by one writer as 'an incomparable fuel' which also 'has the smoothness of marble, the texture of porcelain, the glossiness of bronze . . . the cleanliness of glass'. Cannel carving was an active local craft in the 17th and 18th centuries.

Canteen. The term dates from the late 17th century when it applied to a travelling case of shagreen or other material containing individual set of silver knife, fork and spoon, with beaker and condiment box. More recently used to describe a

Example of a Casket

Caster for sugar, pepper, etc.

set of silver, or plated, knives, forks and spoons for a number of people, housed in a case.

Capstan Salt. Salt-cellar so named since it is shaped like a ship's capstan.

Caskets. Small coffers made and decorated in an infinite variety of forms from the 13th or 14th century. The earliest of these were of Sicilian origin, probably made by Arabic craftsmen.

Cast. The end-product of molten metal or plaster poured into a shaped mould.

Cast-iron. Iron with a high carbon content, hard and brittle in character.

Caster. Sugar, pepper and mustard containers, made of silver and sometimes of brass or pewter, cylindrical or pear-shaped, with pierced covers.

Castwork. Cast sections, such as handles, feet, spouts and finials soldered to the main body of a silver vessel.

Cauldron. Colloquially known in certain parts as 'crocks'. In reality a kettle, made from earliest times in bronze and, from the 16th century, in cast-iron.

Censer. Incense burner suspended from chains, used from medieval times.

127

Chafing dish

Chalice

Centre-piece. A version of the epergne (q.v.), a silver table centre in the shape of a wirework or pierced basket on a foliage or figure stem. Found in a variety of decorative forms.

Chafing Dish. Obsolete term for a dish for hot foods.

Chafing-stand. Brazier or spirit-lamp stand for chafing-dish.

Chalice. Shallow vessel on high stem and circular or polygonal foot to contain wine in the celebration of Mass. Also called Communion Cup.

Chamber Candlestick. Dating from the 17th century, in silver or brass. Short, with circular base and handle, sometimes with extinguishers and, later, snuffers carried in aperture in the stem.

Charger. Also known as Sideboard Dish. Used for display and presentation. Large circular dish usually enriched by engraved or embossed armorials.

Chasing. Term for the working over of rough-cast; also for relief decoration on silver, raised by surface hammering.

Cheese-scoop. Cheese server, having a short curved blade with silver shaft and, in the late 18th century, ivory or wood handles. Later examples have silver handles.

Chestnut Servers. Urn-shaped vessel with short, slender stem and spreading foot, ring handles and domed cover. Made both in Britannia metal and copper alloy.

Chiselled (or cut) Steel. An art practised in the locksmith's and gunsmith's trade. In the 17th and 18th centuries in Brescia snuffboxes, scissors, tweezers, etc., were fashioned by this art; in Paris, in addition, sword and gun furniture; in Russia candlesticks, caskets and whole mantlepieces; in England, among other things, buckles and cheap jewellery.

Chocolate Pot. As distinct from the silver coffee-pot, has detachable or sliding cover finial for insertion of swizzlestick.

Chop Dish. Flat, two-handled oblong plate or dish; made 1750 to 1800.

Chopin. Scottish one and a half Imperial pint wine measure.

Ciborium. Standing bowl and cover to contain the Host or, in the Protestant church, the Communion bread.

Cire-perdue. Traditional method of casting bronze with the use of wax.

Cloisonné. One of the most ancient forms of enamelling. Different colours were applied between thin metal plates laid on edge on a foundation plaque.

Close Nailing. Brass-headed nails applied in close line formation to secure leather covering to chests and other upholstery on chair seats and backs.

Charger   **Chocolate Pot**   **Ciborium**

Coffee-pot

Cream Jug

Coach and Post Horn. Frequently made of copper. The distinction is that coach horns, which vary from 30″ to 54″ in length, are more funnel-shaped, the post horns narrower in the tube and more 'flared' at the wide end. Both are traditionally made in a single straight tube.

Coffee-pot. Introduced c. 1680. Early examples in straight, tapered form, later in polygonal form. Pear-shape, c. 1750, and in form of vase in the Adam period.

Columbine Cups. Standing cups which were required to be made by candidates for admission as Masters to the Nuremberg Goldsmith's Guild during the second half of the 16th century.

Communion Cup. See CHALICE.

Copper Blank. Paper thin metal serving as a base for enamels.

Corkscrew Thumbpiece. American term for twisted thumbpiece on tankards. Of Dutch origin.

Cran. Iron trivet fire-fitment to support kettle, girdle-plate, etc.

Cream Jug. From 19th century, integral part of tea service. From Queen Anne to George II period—plain pitcher-shaped; mid-18th century, pear-shaped on three legs; later, vase shape and, thereafter, flat-bottomed.

Cruet Frame. See CRUETS. Frame with open rings and side

handles to hold condiment bottles. Later versions were oblong in shape.

Cruets. Water and wine vessels for use at the Eucharist. Also, condiment bottles in frames. The first examples of silver frames date from Queen Anne.

Cup, Coconut. Found from medieval times to the 19th century. Standing cup with bowl, sometimes with cover made from the nut, with silver straps, lip and foot. 18th-century examples sometimes have small silver feet.

Cup, Font-shaped. 16th-century circular wine cup on spreading feet.

Coconut Cup   **Font-shaped Cup**   **Standing Cup**

Cup, Ostrich Egg. Standing cup with egg bowl and upper part inset in cover. In 16th century, with highly ornamented straps; later examples with plain mounts.

Cup, Standing. Large ceremonial or decorative cup on high stem and foot found in many styles. After 17th century, replaced by the two-handled cup on low foot without stem. Mostly made with covers.

131

Steeple Cup

Wine Cup

Cupping-bowl

Cup, Steeple. Standing cup surmounted by obelisk or pyramid finial. Found in time of James I and into reign of Charles I.

Cup, Wager. Belongs to Charles II period, but copies made in 18th and early 19th centuries. Double cup in shape of skirted woman swinging cup above her head. The skirt forms a second cup. To satisfy the wager each cup had to be drained without a spill.

Cup, Wine. Small goblet on high stem. Also known as Grace cup. Late 16th and 17th century.

Cupping-bowl. Shallow, circular bowl with handle, believed to have been used for cupping or bleeding, but more probably employed as a porringer, the name by which it is known in America.

Cut Steel. See CHISELLED STEEL.

Cut-cardwork. Flat sheet metal cut into foliage or strap outline and soldered on to a surface to form relief decoration. Of late 17th-century French origin.

Damascening. Encrusting gold and/or silver on iron, steel, brass or copper, an ancient art and one which particularly flourished in Milan in the second half of the 16th century.

Date-letters. FIRST TWO: London; 1558–9, 1716–17. LAST TWO: Sheffield; 1773–4, 1755–6

English sword and knife handles of the 17th century show fine examples of damascening.

Date-letter. Letter of the alphabet found on English silver, denoting the year of the hall-mark.

Decanter Stand. See WINE COASTER.

Dessert Basket. Oval or circular, usually pierced and gilt, in a variety of sizes. Late 18th century.

Dessert Service. Mostly made in the late 18th century and subsequently; plates, dishes and baskets in a gilt version of the contemporary white dinner service, following the same pattern.

Dessert Table Service. Spoons, knives and forks in a gilt version of the white table services; also found with vine, foliage and bacchanalian patterns.

Dinanderie. Name given to range of small brassware, mostly for domestic use, made in Dinant, near Liége, and in the surrounding region in the Middle Ages.

Dinner Service. The term embraces everything—plates, tureens, dishes, etc.—required to furnish a dinner table.

Dipped Enamel. From about 1776 the method of applying enamel to the copper core with a spatula was abandoned in favour of ladling liquid enamel in three layers over the metal and then firing.

Dish Cross. Silver or plated spirit-lamp stand with two adjustable arms revolving round the lamp, 1750–80.

Dish Ring. Originated in Ireland, mid-18th century; also known as 'potato ring'. Circular dish or bowl with sides usually pierced and chased with pastoral or classical motifs.

Douters. Used for extinguishing candles. Unlike snuffers, which have a cutting edge, douters have flat 'blades'.

133

Dram Cup. Two-handled bowl resembling wine taster. Examples after 1720 are rare.

Dredger. Small 18th-century pepper-pot, cylindrical with side scroll handle.

Drip-shield. Wide collar on candlestick between the base and the stem to protect the hand from dripping grease.

Ecuelle

Egg-frame

Drum. Body of flagon, tankard, etc.

Dutch Metal. Substitute for gold-leaf; an alloy of copper and zinc.

Ecuelle. French form of circular, shallow soup-bowl and cover with flat handles and dish stand. The same form is occasionally found in English silver. Late 17th to mid-18th century.

Egg and Dart. Classical motif for borders used by furniture makers and goldsmiths, etc., from 16th century onwards, consisting of alternating ovolos and arrowheads.

Egg and Tongue. Introduced into England in the Renaissance period; alternate ovolos and pointed mouldings repeated to form pattern; usually die-stamped but sometimes chased by hand.

Egg-frame. Frame to hold two or more egg-cups and spoons with, occasionally, a salt-cellar above. Introduced c. 1785.

134

Electro-plate. The result of coating with silver by the electro-lysis process a base metal, usually copper. First patented 1840.

Entrée Dish

Embossing. A generic term to describe relief work on metal.

Enamel. Coloured glass, powdered and fused, used in accordance with a variety of formulae as a decoration for gold, silver or copper.

Enamelled Brassware. A cheap form of enamelling with brass as a base, introduced to England and the Continent in the 17th century. English enamelled brassware is usually referred to as 'Surrey' enamel.

English Plate. Term invented by Sheffield platers to distinguish their method of plating silver on copper from the method of plating on white alloy as practised by the Germans.

Engraving. Flat line decoration incised on a surface with a cutting tool.

Entrée Dish. Dishes having covers with handles which are frequently detachable, allowing the cover to be used as a separate dish. Early examples usually circular or polygonal; later, oblong or even oval, some having silver or plated heater stands.

135

Epergne. Elaborate table centrepiece housing dishes for fruit or sweetmeats.

Etched Metalwork. Acid etching is believed to have been introduced in the second half of the 15th century as a means of decorating armour. It was subsequently applied to a wide variety of objects from cutlery, tools and locks to caskets and clock-cases. The German craftsmen particularly excelled at this form of decoration.

Epergne

Etching. Commonly associated with the print process, some English silver of the 16th century was decorated by this 'bitten-in with acid' technique.

Feather-edge Ornament. Pattern of chased, slanting lines on edge of silver spoon and fork handles.

Feeding Cup. Known also as 'spout cup'. Small saucepan-shaped cup with two handles and spout for feeding children and invalids. From mid-17th century.

Ferronière. Ornament to encircle the head in form of wrought iron chain with a jewel in the centre.

Fiddle Pattern. Pattern applied to table-services (spoons,

**Feather-edge
Ornament**

Fiddle Pattern

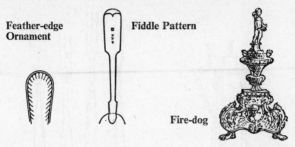

Fire-dog

forks, etc.) from the early 19th century. The broad-topped stems and notched shoulders convey the rough impression of a fiddle.

Fire-dog. In the 16th century many were garnished with silver; a century later they were produced entirely in silver. See ANDIRON.

Fish Slice. Mid-18th century. Early examples elaborately decorated with engraved fish and floral patterns, and finely pierced; later models plainer and made en suite with table services. The accompanying fish fork dates from c. 1800.

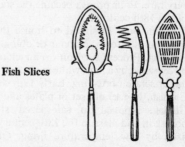

Fish Slices

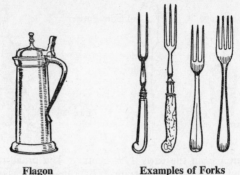

Flagon   Examples of Forks

Fish Strainer. Also called MAZARINE. Flat silver straining plate, pierced, used for fish dishes.

Flagon. Large vessel for serving wine or other liquors; after the 18th century almost exclusively found in ecclesiastical use.

Flat Chasing. Early 18th-century low relief decoration executed by hammering with small blunt tools.

Forks. Silver examples produced prior to the 18th century are very rare. Four prongs became the standard about the middle of the 18th century.

Freedom Box. Designed to house the script conferring the freedom of a town; circular or oblong, gilt or gold.

Frosting. Process used on ornamental figure-work on centre-pieces whereby a matt white surface was produced by acid fuming or scratch brushing. Early 19th century.

Garnish. Household set of plates and dishes.

Gilding. Applied to salt-glazed stoneware, earthenware, porcelain and glass in the 18th century by dint of an emulsion fixed by low temperature firing. Of the various gildings:

138

mercury gilding was introduced about 1785; raised gilding in 1802; liquid gold about 1855; bright burnished gold in 1860; acid gilding in 1863.

Girdle Plate. Scottish. Flat iron plate for baking oat-cakes. (Also GRIDDLE.)

Gold Leaf. Gold beaten into thin sheets.

Grace Cup. See WINE CUP.

Grid-iron. Grid consisting of parallel bars laid across the fire for cooking meat, etc. Later models had refinements for channelling away the gravy and a spout for pouring it out.

Guernsey Measure. Peculiar to Guernsey, in the Channel Islands; a pewter measure with heart-shaped lid and twin acorn thumbpiece.

Hall-marks: London; 1565–72, 1796–1816.   Sheffield; 1792–3, 1799–1800

Hall-mark. Mark of Hall or Assay Office, e.g. leopard's head for London, crown for Sheffield, etc., imposed on silver. The term is loosely used in the plural in reference to all the marks on silver. See also DATE-LETTER.

Hanap. Medieval name for Standing Cup.

Hanoverian Pattern Spoons. Having a central longitudinal ridge on the front and up-curved ends of the stem. From c. 1720–40.

Hash Dish. Circular silver or plated dish with cover and loop or drop-ring handles, often accompanied by frame stand and spirit-lamp. 18th or 19th century.

Typical Hasp

Hasp. Hinged strap with lock to secure door or chest, etc.

Hat Pins. Discs of painted enamel mounted on stamped hat and cloak pins, patented by John Marston and Samuel Bellamy in 1777.

Haystack. Irish pewter tavern measure.

Hollow Ware. Embracing term for pewter flagons, tankards, measures, pots, mugs and beakers.

Holy-water Bucket. Container from which holy water is sprinkled at the beginning of Mass; early examples straight sided, the bombé-vase shape coming into use in the 17th century.

Honey-pot. Made at end of 18th century and into 19th century. Jar in shape of skep beehive with cover and dishstand.

Horse Brasses

140

Horn used as drinking vessel   Hot-water Jug

Horn. Used in medieval times as drinking vessel; ox or buffalo horn with silver and gilt mounts.

Horse Brasses. Decorations in brass of various designs hung on the harness of heavy horses. See also BELL HORSE BRASSES.

Hot-milk Jug. In shape and decoration, smaller version of coffee- or chocolate-pot. Some have egg-shaped body on three feet.

Hot-water Jug. Differs hardly at all from the coffee-pot with which it was contemporary.

Ice Pail. Shaped like a vase or tub, usually fitted with liner

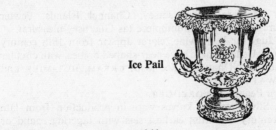

Ice Pail

141

Ink Stand

Jug for beer or wine

and flat rim, commonly made in pairs or sets of four or more from the last quarter of the 18th century, each pail accommodating one bottle. Also called Wine Cooler.

Incense Boat. Vessel made of precious or base metal, or of semi-precious stone mounted in metal, for carrying the incense before it is burnt in the censer.

Inkstand. Early name: STANDISH. In a variety of established forms, but few recorded before 1680. 'Treasury' type: oblong casket with two centrally hinged lids. Glass bottles introduced c. 1765; mahogany desk models with silver tops, 1800 onwards.

Intaglio. Design carved out of surface of gem, rock crystal or glass.

Jersey Measure. From Jersey, Channel Islands. Pewter measure with lid and thumbpiece (as Guernsey measure).

Jugs. Jugs for beer, wine, claret appear from 18th century onwards. Usually these have pear-shaped bodies, with circular feet and scroll handles. See also: CREAM, HOT-MILK and HOT-WATER JUGS.

Kitchen Pepper. See DREDGER.

Knife. Silver-handled knives were in production from late 17th century onwards; earliest sets with tapering round or polygonal handle, followed by pistol handle and, later, thin stamped sheet metal handle filled with resin. Made en suite with rest of table-service, 1800 onwards.

Knulling. Mid-18th-century design for borders and handles, consisting of short fluting of irregular outline.

Ladle, Cream. Small, with curved handle, similar to a sugar-sifter.

Ladle, Punch. Long-handled ladle, the earlier handles being of silver, the 18th-century handles usually of wood or whale-bone. The bowls were sometimes inset with or beaten out of a silver coin. Also known as Toddy-ladle.

Ladle, Sauce. Has a deep, circular bowl and curved stem. In the mid-18th century examples occur with shell bowls and foliage or bird's-head handles.

Ladle, Soup. Similar to sauce ladle, but with long stem, earlier examples having hooked ends.

Latten. Yellow alloy of copper and zinc.

Limmel. Metal scrapings or filings.

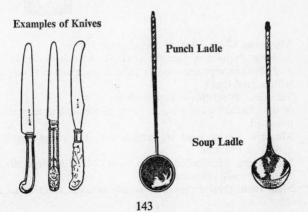

Examples of Knives

Punch Ladle

Soup Ladle

Limoges Enamel. Limoges, in France, was a famous centre of enamelling in the Middle Ages. During the Renaissance the beauty of their enamels was unrivalled.

Loving Cup. General term for twin-handled cup. Original function as a toasting cup.

Lug. Flat handle of a quaich (Scottish pewter drinking bowl), from the Scottish word for an ear.

Mace. Emblem of authority (civic, university or state) derived from medieval weapon. Examples date from the 15th century onwards.

Mazer

Tavern Measure

Mannheim Gold. Alloy of copper, zinc and tin.

Matting. Popular surface for tankard and cup bodies in the mid-17th century; achieved by punching surface of silverware with burred tool.

Mazarine. Silver fish-straining plate.

Mazer. Drinking-bowl made from maple and usually silver mounted.

Measure. Vessel used in taverns for dispensing standard quantities of liquid.

Meat Plate. Also called Dinner plate. Made in large sets in 18th and early 19th centuries.

Meat Dish. Oval dishes in a variety of sizes from 10 to 30 inches long, in successive periods from 1730 with rims shaped and gadrooned, beaded and moulded.

Mercury Gilding. See GILDING.

Midband. American term to describe moulded band below centre of silver tankard. Introduced early 18th century.

Monstrance. A piece of church plate in which the Host is displayed.

Moulding. Mould castings. Also cast or hammered border or girdle based on architectural principle of convex and concave members in a variety of arrangements.

Muffineer

Mounts. Metal strips binding the exposed edges of the enamel to hide the copper core.

Muffineer. A form of caster, used for sprinkling salt on muffins.

Mug. Small-handled drinking vessel. Shapes vary with period: late 17th century, belly-shaped body with cylindrical neck; late 18th century, hooped barrel form; 19th century, return of shaped form.

Mustard-pot. Until well into the 18th century mustard was taken dry from casters and mixed on the plate. The oval or spherical pot, with glass liner, was introduced to accommodate mustard in its liquid form.

Mutchkin. Scottish wine measure to contain three-quarters of an Imperial pint.

Nickel Silver. Silver plated on white alloy.

Niello. Black metallic amalgam of sulphur added to copper, silver, lead, etc., for filling engraved lines in silver or other metal as decoration.

Nutmeg Grater. Oval, circular or cylindrical boxes with steel grater under cover or down the side; also in hanging form with curved grater at front. Dating from the late 17th century and onwards.

Pilgrim Bottle

Paten

Oil and Vinegar Frame. Small stand with ring frames for glass oil and vinegar cruets. Successor to the larger cruet forms, and dating from the early 18th century onwards.

Ovolo Base. Base of hollow ware formed by projecting mould, ing or quarter-curve; found on pewter flagons of the 17th century.

Pap-boat. Or pap-dish. Shallow bowl with tapering lip or spout for feeding infants. Examples in silver survive from the early 18th century; also made of other materials.

Parcel-gilt. Plate partially gilded.

Paten. Small silver, silver-gilt or gold plate used for serving the wafer or Communion bread.

Pea-pod Designs. Engraved designs employing stylised leaf-shapes resembling pea-pods for the use of goldsmiths for the decoration of enamelled gold miniature cases, etc. From second quarter of the 17th century.

Peg Tankard. Rare 17th-century silver tankard, the interior of which has a vertical line of studs acting as a drinking measure.

Perfume-burner. Rare 17th-century pierced metal vase on scroll feet.

Pewter. Grey alloy of tin and lead or other metal, resembling lead in appearance when dull, but capable of receiving a high polish.

Pied de Biche. See SPOON, PIED DE BICHE.

Pierced Work. Fretwork decoration cut with saw, found in lattice and diaper designs.

Pilgrim Bottle. Derivative of medieval leather bottle; long-necked with stopper and chains made in silver for display purposes in late 17th and early 18th centuries.

Pin Cushion. Silver-framed examples survive from the late 17th century.

Pinchbeck. Gold-like alloy of copper and zinc used in cheap jewellery (named after Christopher Pinchbeck, London watch and toy maker, c. 1730).

Plaquettes. Comparable in a sense with medals except that they are one-sided rather than double-sided, and square, oblong or oval rather than round. Cast in lead, silver and bronze and depicting on their surface mythological, historical or religious subjects, they were first used in the 15th century to decorate household utensils and furniture. Later became collectors' pieces.

Plate. Generic term for wrought silver or gold. Later applied to Sheffield wares and electro-plate.

Plateau. Plinth or stand, usually with mirror centre for table centrepiece. Sometimes arranged in sections to run whole length of table. Early 19th century.

Potato Ring   **Rosewater Ewer and Dish**

Potato Ring. Also known as DISH RING. Circular silver dish with straight or incurved sides bearing classical motifs. 18th century Irish.

Pottle-pot. Quart pot.

Presentoir. 15th-century serving knife with broad blade and square or rounded point.

Pricking. Needle-point engraving, largely used in the 16th and 17th centuries for working armorials and inscriptions on silver.

Prince's Metal. Brass alloy tinged to the colour of gold by a process initiated in the 17th century.

Punched Work. Mid-17th-century practice of embossing with blunt punches in primitive floral designs.

Puzzle Cup. See CUP, WAGER.

Quaich. Scottish drinking-bowl in silver or pewter, with two handles. From early 17th century.

Raising. The process of shaping a hollow vessel from sheet silver by hammering on a wood block. During the process the silver, hardened by the hammering, is repeatedly softened as required by being brought to red-heat.

Reeding. As fluting but with the ornament in relief.

148

Standing Salt

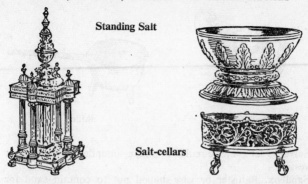

Salt-cellars

Repoussé Work. Embossed design produced by hammering a malleable material, such as silver, copper or iron, on the reverse side.

Rosewater Ewer and Dish or Basin. For washing the fingers at table. Dishes circular or oval, ewers chiefly in vase- or helmet-shapes. Examples survive from the early 16th century onwards.

Sadware. Pewterers' term for plates, dishes and chargers.

Salad Servers. Spoons with flattened bowls and forks with deep, wide prongs, first made 1800.

Salamander. Used for browning bread, cake, etc.; long, wrought-iron handle with thick round or oblong disc at one end which was held over the fire until red-hot.

Salt, Standing. Principal piece on medieval banqueting high table; in Elizabethan times of pedestal- or bell-form, richly decorated. Early 17th-century models have 'steeple' finials.

Salt-cellar. First known as Trencher Salt. In 18th century, shallow, circular bowl on moulded base; later on three or four feet. Glass liners introduced *c.* 1765.

Sauceboat

Skillet

Salver. Flat plate, circular in shape, intended to bear other vessels.

Sandbox. Baluster or vase-shaped pot to contain sand for sprinkling on wet ink; found separately or as part of inkstand.

Sauceboat. Early oval-moulded base was later followed by scroll or hoof feet. Handles in shape of dolphins, eagles' heads, etc. Early 18th century; revived early 19th century.

Saucepan. Succeeded the Skillet, a form of saucepan on three feet, in the 18th century.

Scent-bottle. Existed in 17th century toilet services; in 18th century, smaller and pear-shaped with chased or engraved decoration.

Seal-box. Flat circular or oval box to contain the seal attached to such important documents as Royal warrants, etc.; cover embossed or engraved with armorials.

Second-course Dish. Circular dish for serving entremets and puddings. 18th and early 19th century.

Shaving-dish and Jug. Rare; some pewter examples exist. Dish, oval with notch at one side; jug with cover and thumb-piece. Late 17th century.

Shaving-pot. Cylindrical or tapering vessel with detachable ivory or wooden handle, stand and spirit lamp. Late 18th century.

Sheffield Plate. Invented by Thomas Bolsover, c. 1743; first really effective substitute for wrought silver. First used for small items such as buttons, etc., but after the middle of the 18th century constituted a rival to silver in the production of every type of vessel.

Shell. Representation of scallop-shell for holding butter and for other uses. From the beginning of the 18th century.

Shell for butter, etc.   Example of Skirt-base   Snuffer

Shell Thumbpiece. Found on tankards; formed of ribbed or plain scallop shell.

Sideboard Dish. See CHARGER.

Silver-gilt. The application of a gold surface on silver, traditionally by a process of painting on an amalgam of mercury and gold. The modern method is by electro-gilding.

Skewer. Meat skewers date from the early 18th century. The ring or shell top acts as a grip.

Skillet. See SAUCEPAN.

Skirt-base. Found sometimes on late 17th-century pewter flagons; a wide spreading base.

Snuffer. Instrument for trimming candle-wicks, in the shape of scissors.

151

Snuffer stand

Caddy Spoon

Snuffer Stand. 17th-century upright container for snuffer, replaced by tray in the early 18th century.

Snuffer Tray. Oblong or oval tray for holding snuffer (q.v.), some with feet and scroll or ring handle.

Soap Box. Spherical box on moulded base to contain soap in the shape of a ball.

Soufflé Dish. Cylindrical silver or plated bowl with liner. From early 19th century.

Spelter. Zinc. Used in the 19th century for the manufacture of cheap decorative objects.

Spit. For roasting meat. The meat was pierced by a metal bar which was then placed on cobirons before the fire. The bar was rotated by a system of pulleys and chains or ropes manipulated by human or animal power (i.e. 'turnspit') or by various ingenious mechanical means culminating eventually in clockwork (i.e. 'spit-jacks').

Spool Salt. Salt cellar in form of flattened hour-glass.

Spoon, Apostle. Having as its finial full-length representation of Christ or an apostle. Examples date from late 15th century to Charles II period.

Spoon, Caddy. Short-handled spoon for measuring tea from

152

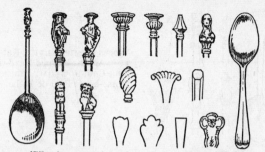

Spoons (Silver). LEFT: Apostle. RIGHT: Old English Pattern.
TOP: Two Apostle; Two Seal Top; Stump;Maidenhead.
CENTRE: Onslow Pattern; Wrythen-top; Slip-top.
BOTTOM: Two Lion Sejant; Two Trefid; Puritan; King's Pattern

the caddy. Made from 1780 onwards in a variety of representational forms (e.g. jockey cap, hand, leaf, etc.).

Spoon, Dessert. As table spoon but smaller. Introduced early 18th century.

Spoon, Diamond. Multi-sided; pewter.

Spoon, Egg. First accompanied egg frames, later became part of the table service. From late 18th century.

Spoon, Gravy. Long-handled spoon, similar to basting spoon.

Spoon, King's Pattern. Shaped stems with waisted hour-glass tops, decorated with scrolls, shells, etc. Early 19th century.

Spoon, Lion Sejant. Surmounted by seated lion supporting a shield. Also Lion Rampant. From 15th to early 17th century.

Spoon, Maidenhead. Finial in shape of long-haired female head surmounting Gothic foliage, traditionally associated with the Virgin Mary. 15th to 17th century.

Spoon, Marrow. Two versions: one, tablespoon with marrow bowl in place of handle; the other, long, narrow spoon, usually double-ended. Both intended for eating bone-marrow. Early 18th century and onwards.

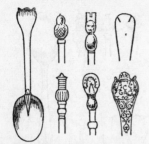

Spoons (Pewter). LEFT: Rat-tail.
TOP: Acorn; Horned Head-dress;
Split End. BOTTOM: Baluster;
Horse-hoof; Pied de Biche

Spoon, Mulberry. See SPOON, STRAINING.

Spoon, Mustard. Egg-shaped bowl preceded by deep circular bowl. From mid-18th century.

Spoon, Old English Pattern. Plain form with flat stem spreading slightly to rounded end. Common from mid-18th century onwards.

Spoon, Olive. See SPOON, STRAINING.

Spoon, Onslow Pattern. Rare mid-18th- century form. Upper third of stem decorated with radiating fluting and cast and applied corkscrew-like scroll tops.

Spoon, Pied de Biche. Stem-shaped like a hind's hoof, with split end.

Spoon, Puritan. Earliest form of English flat-stemmed spoon. Mid-17th century.

Spoon, Queen's Pattern. As KING'S PATTERN, but with decoration solely on upper surface of stem and without shell on bowl.

Spoon, Rat-tail. Stem tapering down back of bowl.

Spoon, Salt. Found in a variety of forms, including shovel and small version of rat-tail. Later conformed to main table service patterns.

Spoon, Seal-top. 15th century to Charles II period; so called for its flat seal-like finial. Hexagonal stem.

Spoon, Slipped in the Stalk. With stem cut off on the slant. Pre-Commonwealth.

Spoon, Snuff. Miniature versions of contemporary spoons kept in snuff-boxes and étuis.

Spoon, Straining. Spoon with pierced bowl; a large version for use with gravy, a small one for removing leaves from teacups. Also called Mulberry Spoon or Olive Spoon.

Spoon, Stump-top. Octagonal stem swelling at end and diminishing to flattened point. 17th century; rare.

Spoon, Table. Larger version of Dessert Spoon.

Straining Spoon

Spoon, Tea. Sets date almost exclusively from post-1700. The mid-18th century marked a departure from the spoon's conformity with larger contemporary spoons, examples being found with foliage stems and bowls, shell bowls and stamped devices on bowl backs.

Spoon Tray. Oblong dish usually with scalloped and fluted or moulded rims for holding teaspoons, there being no saucers. Early 18th century.

Spoon, Trefid or Trifid. Also known as PIED DE BICHE or SPLIT END. Normally with rat-tailed bowls. Late 17th century, with flat stem and likeness to cleft hoof at top.

Spoon, Wrythen-top. Medieval; rare form. Spirally-fluted ovoid finial.

Stake. Anvil or iron tongue used for shaping silverware.

Stamped Gold. Stamped thin gold sheet used for cheap jewellery mounts, late 18th and 19th centuries.

Stamped Work. Relief work on metal produced by hammering from reverse side into an intaglio-cut die. Used in the 16th century and onwards.

Steeple Cup. Standing cup with obelisk or pyramid finial.

Sterling Standard. Normal British standard for wrought plate (925 parts of fine silver in every 1000 parts of wrought metal). In force 1300 to 1696, when replaced by Britannia Standard; restored in 1720.

Stoning. The procedure of polishing silver with an emery-stone.

Strapwork. Patterns of interlaced ribbon and scrollwork mixed with foliage and floral decoration, engraved or repoussé. Common in 16th-century work. Also applied to ribbing and scrollwork derived from the cut-cardwork of the Huguenot school.

Strawberry-dish. 'Saucers' with punched decoration in the earlier examples and scalloped borders in the later. 17th and early 18th century.

Striking Plate. Metal plate on door frame to receive the bolt when it is shot by the key.

Sucket-fork. For eating fruit; two-pronged with a spoon at the reverse end.

Sugar-basin. Part of tea service from the end of the 18th century onwards; oblong, circular or oval with two handles.

Sugar-basket. Predecessor of the sugar-basin; pierced or plain with swing handle, the former having glass liner.

Sugar-bowl. Circular or polygonal; in early 18th century, individual piece, later part of set with two tea-caddies in casket.

Sugar-nippers. From George I and II periods, early form of sugar-tongs with scrolling stems and shell grips.

Sugar-sifter. Small ladle with pierced bowl. Mid-18th century.

Sugar-tongs. In early 18th century in form of miniature fire-tongs; later models in spring bow form.

Sugar-basket   Sugar-bowl   Sugar-nippers

Sweetmeat Basket. Mid-18th century. Oval or circular basket; early examples mostly pierced with floral borders, later examples solid with engraved decoration.

Table Service. Matched set of tableware.

Tankard. Single-handed drinking vessel for beer. See also MUG.

Taper Box. Container for coiled sealing-wax taper; cylindrical with handle and hole in lid. From c. 1700 onwards.

Sugar-tongs   Tankards: LEFT: silver; RIGHT: pewter

Tea Caddy   **Tea-kettle**

Tea Caddy. Tea container found in a variety of forms: rectangular, octagonal, vase-shaped, etc., in numerous kinds of wood or silver. Usually with locks and with inner compartments for different kinds of tea.

Tea Service. Few examples of matching tea-sets are to be found in England before 1785, although there is evidence that Scotland was ahead in this respect.

Tea-kettle. Precursor of the tea-urn, in form of teapot with stands for charcoal or spirit-lamp, dating from c. 1690.

Tea-tray. The large double-handled oval or oblong tray was introduced c. 1780.

Tea Service

Tea-urn. Successor to the tea-kettle. Vase-shaped hot-water urn originally with internal compartment for red-hot heating iron, later used in conjunction with methylated spirit lamp. From c. 1765.

Teacup. A few silver examples without handles survive from the beginning of the 18th century.

Tea-urn

Teacup-stand. Circular dish with detachable frame for holding porcelain cups. Early 18th century.

Teapot. The more familiar squat circular type was introduced in the early 19th century, accompanied by sugar-basin and cream-jug to match. Earlier, from the 17th century onwards, the teapot assumed in succession a pear, spherical, and oval shape.

'Thistle' Cup. Scottish. Resemblance to teacup, with S-handle and lobe-like decorations round the body. From the end of the 17th century.

Threading. Narrow engraved lines (one or two) as border on stem of silver spoon, fork and other small items.

Thumbpiece or Billet. Protrusion above hinge of lid of covered vessel to allow the lid to be raised by the thumb. Various types are to be found, including: BAR AND HEART, BUD, CHAIR-BACK, HAMMER-HEAD, LOVE BIRD, etc.

Toast-rack. Usually found on four feet with ring handle; early examples have detachable wires on oval base. Introduced c. 1770.

Toasted Cheese Dish. Oval or oblong dish, having hinged cover and hot-water compartment below. Late 18th century.

Toasted Cheese Dish

Tobacco-box. Circular or oval box with hinged or detachable lid. Often finely engraved with armorials or monograms. Late 17th century onwards.

Toddy-ladle. See LADLE, PUNCH.

Toilet Service. Sets of toilet-boxes, mirror, candlesticks, brushes, etc., sumptuously decorated. Post-Restoration until mid-18th century.

Tôle. French word for sheet iron. Commonly used to describe painted tinware.

Touch. An official mark stamped on pewter.

Touch-plate. Soft sheet of pewter on which the pewterer's touch was struck. See TOUCH.

Toy Silver. Miniature representations of wrought plate items for use in dolls' houses and as children's playthings.

Transfer Printing. Process of conveying a design from an engraved copper plate to a smooth surface such as enamel by means of a paper transfer. One engraving could in this way be reproduced on hundreds of surfaces.

Trivet

Tumbler Cup

Trencher Salt. Small salt-cellar standing on its own with solid sides but without feet. In use from c. 1630. See also SALT-CELLAR.

Trivet. General term used to cover a variety of stands on which cooking utensils were placed before the fire. (Strictly 3-legged).

Tumbler Cup. Small, plain drinking bowl, straight-sided with rounded base. Mid-17th century onwards.

Two-handled Cup. Normally found with cover and frequently used as 'loving cup'. Late 17th century. See also CUP, STANDING.

Vase. Richly decorated sets of vases date from the Restora-

Two-handled Cup

Decorated Vase

tion, when they were used for chimney display. In the late 18th century the classical form was much in vogue.

Vegetable Dish. Circular or oval in shape with cover and deep sides. Introduced late 18th century. See also HASH DISH.

Venison Dish. Similar to meat-dish with channels and well for collecting gravy.

Vermeil. French. Silver gilt (q.v.).

Waiter. Smaller version of the salver; used for carrying wine-glass, letters, etc. In 18th century often in pairs en suite with salver.

Water-leaf Ornament. Late 18th and early 19th-century plate ornament in form of large leaf without ribs.

Wine Cistern. Large oval vessel, highly decorated, sometimes on separate feet, for keeping bottles in ice or water. Charles II period to mid-18th century.

Wine Cistern

Wine Coaster. Bottle or decanter holder for table use, circular in shape, having, as a rule, turned wood base and pierced or solid silver sides. Occurring in pairs, sets of four, or more. From mid-18th century.

Wine Cooler. See ICE PAIL.

Wine Fountain. Large urn with tap, found in late 17th and early 18th centuries with matching wine cisterns (q.v.).

Wine-bottle Stand. For holding early form of glass wine bottle; oval bowl on moulded base.

Wine-labels

Wine-funnel. Equipped with detachable strainer for decanting. Circular stands with domed centres often accompanied the funnels.

Wine-label. Made in silver and enamel and pierced or chased with the name of the wine, hung usually with a chain round the neck of a decanter. See also BOTTLE TICKETS.

Wine-taster. Shallow, circular bowl, with or without handle(s) and with slightly domed centre. Mid-17th century onwards.

Wrigglework. Used more in pewter than in silverwork. Zig-zag line, used particularly in the 17th century in conjunction with line engraving. Effected by side-to-side manipulation of a gouge.

Example of Wrigglework

PART FOUR

Bijouterie

After-cast. Bronze figure or object produced from a mould of an existing model.

Amorini. Cupids, frequently used as decorative motif in the late 17th century.

Amulet. Object worn as charm against evil.

Aquamanile. Term covers bronze ewers used to pour water over the hands after each course of a meal. From 13th century.

Armorial Fan. 18th-century ivory or tortoiseshell fan decorated with coat of arms or crest.

Automata. Mechanically operated figures, dating from the early 18th century.

Bead-work. The use of coloured beads as a surface decoration on a variety of articles such as trays, baskets, looking-glass frames, etc. From 17th century.

Bergaute. Lacquer tray.

Egyptian Amulet

Typical Aquamanile

Bead-work tray

Bonbonnière

Bird-organ. Small mechanical instrument, operated by bellows, intended to encourage a bird to sing. Also called Serinette or Turlutaine.

Bonbonnières. Small sweetmeat boxes in gold, silver, porcelain or enamelled copper. Also called Comfit boxes.

Bridal Fans. Finely decorated fans intended for presentation to maids of honour and women guests at a wedding. 18th century.

Brin. See FAN BLADE.

Brisé Fan. Leafless fan. Early examples composed solely of flexible ivory, tortoiseshell or horn sticks; by the end of the 18th century, bone, scented sandalwood, laburnum wood and steel were used.

Cabriole Fan. Often decorated with picture of the two-wheeled carriage of that name, the occupant being the owner of the fan. 1770–90.

Brisé Fan

Callot Figures. Jacques Callot (1592–1635) was a French engraver. These figures, made in porcelain, silver or gold, represented the bizarre characters of his drawings.

Cameo. Gem, shell, or imitation material carved in relief. Many fine cameos were cut by the Romans.

Castleford Chess-men. Made in representation of George III and Queen Charlotte, among other models, by David Dunderdale between 1795 and 1821. Originally of vitrified stoneware, these figures have been widely copied in various materials.

Examples of Cameos.   Castleford Chess-men: King and Queen

Chatelaine. Chains holding keys, watch, scissors, etc., formerly worn hanging from woman's girdle or belt.

Chess-boards. Some of the finest chess-boards were made from 1660, with parquetry work in exotic woods and ivory.

Chess-men. From the Middle Ages, when chess-men were sometimes of ivory, encrusted with gold and jewels, numerous materials have been employed. Silver was used in the 18th century, also porcelain.

Chicken Skin. Vellum employed in the 18th century for fan mounts, prepared from the skins of new-born lambs.

Church Fans. Fans decorated with Biblical subjects conveying a moral. 18th century.

Chatelaine

Detail of a wooden Chess-board (1700)

Cochins. Small tablets illustrative of contemporary events, named after their inventor.

Colfichet. Small, late 18th-century Italian embroidered pictures worked in silk on paper.

Comfit Box. See BONBONNIÈRES.

Crown Paperweight. Having coloured canes radiating in straight lines from the top.

Dandies' Sticks. Walking sticks sported by the 19th-century dandies, in a variety of woods with heads of Moors, Turks or Chinese carved for the stick knobs.

Draughts or Checkers. Earliest English description of the game dates from 1566.

Dandies' Sticks

167

Easter Egg by Fabergé   **Typical Etuis**

Easter Eggs. Many beautiful Easter Eggs, containing jewelled objects, were made by Fabergé, the Russian jeweller. See FABERGÉ, PETER CARL (Part 7).

Etui. Small pocket case for sewing materials; also for medical needs and for implements such as a knife, fork, spoon, etc., made in a variety of materials.

Fan Blade. Also known as a brin. The lower ornamental part of an inner stick of a fan.

Fan Guard. The two outer sticks of a fan.

Fan Mounts. Also known as leaves. Made of vellum, chicken skin (q.v.), silk, lace or paper, they unite the upper part of the sticks of a fan.

Fan Pivot. The rivet on the handle end of a fan joining the sticks and enabling them to be opened and shut.

Fan Sticks. These form the framework extending from the pivot to the perimeter of the fan.

Fausse-montre. As the name suggests, a false watch. It was a custom in the 18th century to carry a watch at one end of a Macaroni, or hookless chatelaine (q.v.), and a fausse-montre at the other.

Feathered Fans. Early Victorian import from China; fans painted and decorated with feathers.

'Fruit' Paperweight. Paperweight within which the canes are formed to represent fruit.

Georgette. Snuff-box made in the style of the 18th-century Parisian goldsmith, Jean George.

Gesso. Plaster of Paris or gypsum prepared for use in modelling or as a ground for painting.

'Fruit' Paperweight   Hen and Chickens money-box

Gros-point. Type of cross-stitch embroidery worked on woven canvas.

Guard Chain. Chain worn round the neck from which were hung keys and other articles.

Gypciere. Type of medieval purse.

Hat Badge. Derived from enamelled and jewelled badges worn by medieval pilgrims.

Hen and Chickens. Motif used on money-boxes, being emblems of Providence.

Japan Work. Lacquer work imported from the East until the beginning of the 18th century when it began to be made in England. Items of furniture including screens, mirrors, clock-cases, etc. were japanned.

Jaseron Chain. Venetian gold chain from which was suspended a cross or pendant. Early 19th century.

Kakemono. Japanese picture which, like a wall-map, is rolled up when not hung on the wall.

Kinji. Japanese lacquer-work technique.

Kirikane. Japanese lacquer-work technique.

Lacquer. Natural sap of a tree used since ancient times in China and Japan as protective and decorative varnish, usually applied in thin layers to wooden articles, or inlaid on metal wares. Imitation lacquer, prepared from resin, lac or shellac, was introduced in Europe in the 17th century.

Lacquer Work. See Japan work

Leontine Chain. 19th-century gold watch chain.

Loggerhead. Circular inkstand with wide, fat base.

Macaroni. See FAUSSE-MONTRE.

Manchette. 19th-century bracelet.

Marcasite. Iron pyrites mechanically fashioned like precious stones.

Mechanical Birds. Elegant 'toys' sometimes fitted into snuff-boxes, watches, etc., which could be made to sing. See also AUTOMATA.

Mechanical Draughtsman. Automata constructed to draw or write. See also AUTOMATA.

Mechanical Bird

Mechanical Draughtsman

Medallion Fan

Musical Clock

Mechanical Pictures. Framed pictures, the elements of which could be 'activated'. See also AUTOMATA.

Medallion Fans. Fans with three medallion subjects painted on the silk mount. 1770–90.

Merline. See BIRD-ORGAN.

Miniature Automata. The Swiss excelled at the manufacture of these ingenious 'activated' contrivances, dancing figures in a musical box, watches with disappearing singing birds, etc. See also AUTOMATA.

Minuet Fan. See BRISÉ FAN.

Mon. Japanese name for badge or emblem.

Monte à Cage. Descriptive of elegant framework in which fine snuff-boxes, etuis, etc., were mounted.

Mourning Fans. Fans painted in black and grey overlaid with white.

Mushroom Paperweight. Paperweight in which canes are raised in form of a sheaf.

Musical Clocks. Made in Europe since the 14th century. Some had a repertoire of tunes, which might be played on bells or an organ activated either by hand or automatically at the strike.

171

Musical Novelties. Musical movements attached to a wide variety of articles from tankards and scent bottles to cigar and cigarette boxes. Especially popular in Victorian days.

Musical Snuff-boxes. Snuff-boxes incorporating a musical box. Mostly from the early 19th century.

Musician (Automata). Activated figures of musicians or group of musicians. See also AUTOMATA.

Musical Novelties: Musical seal. Musician (Automata).
Example of Netsuke

Nashiji. Japanese lacquer-work technique.

Nef. Vessel in the form of a ship dating from the Middle Ages, when it contained a gentleman's napkin, knife and spoon. Jugs and cups were made in the same form in the 16th century.

Netsuke. Carved or otherwise ornamented piece of ivory sometimes worn by Japanese as bob or button on a cord by which articles are suspended from a girdle.

Orrery. See PLANETARIUM.

Paillons. Spangles shaped and set in transparent enamel on small boxes, etuis, etc.

Paktong. Alloy of copper, nickel and zinc resembling silver when polished. Also called Tutenag.

Panharmonicon. Mechanical orchestra constructed by J. N. Maelzel (1772–1838).

Paperweight. Heavy piece of clear glass, roughly in the shape of a bun, of which there are innumerable variations in terms of the enclosed pattern which is of coloured glass.

Peepshow. Portable cabinet with eye-pieces through which the scenery contained in it (cut out and placed in perspective) could be seen stereoscopically.

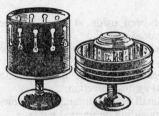 

Peepshows: LEFT: Zoetrope. RIGHT: Phenakistoscope.   **Piqué étui**

Pipe Kiln. Wrought iron frame in which a clay 'churchwarden' pipe was placed in the oven to clean.

Pipe Rack. Stand for clay pipes.

Pipe Tray. Designed to hold 'churchwarden' pipes.

Piqué. Tortoiseshell either inlaid or overlaid with gold or silver cut sheet or pinhead as decoration for etuis and numerous other small articles.

Planetarium. Model of planetary system the elements of which may be set in motion either by a handle or by clock. Also known as Orrery.

Plaster Silhouette. Plaster was a common base for the painting of silhouettes in the 18th and early 19th centuries.

Playing Cards.
LEFT: 1707–8.
RIGHT: 1801–15

Playing Cards. They have been made in many European countries for some five hundred years.

Polychrome. Work of art executed in many colours; special application to statuary.

Pomander. Small container for carrying mixed aromatic substances as a preservation against infection.

Pouncebox or Pouncepot. Small bottle containing fine powder used to prevent ink from spreading on unsized paper.

Pricket Candlestick. Earliest form of candlestick in which candle was secured on an upstanding spike.

Punch Kettle. Similar to a large teapot, from which hot punch was served.

Pomander

Pricket Candlestick

Example of a Rasp   **Quizzing Fan**   **Sand Glass**

Puzzle Fans. So constructed as to show two or four pictures according to how they were handled. Mid-18th century.

Quatrecouleurs. The combined use of different colours of gold, obtained by altering the balance of the alloy, in decoration.

Quillwork. Or paper filigree. Designs made from paper strips variously manipulated.

Quizzing Fans. Fans with peep-holes, and later quizzing glasses, to enable the owner to see what was going on without prejudice to her modesty.

Ramponneau. Barrel-shaped box.

Rasp. A grater. Many tobacco-rasps were made in ivory.

Salt Kit. Jar for storing salt.

Samovar. Russian tea-urn.

Sand Glass. Twin bulbs of glass on the principle of the old egg-timer through which sand passes in a measured time.

Sardonyx. Variety of onyx with white layers alternating with sand (yellow and orange cornelian). From Sardinia.

Scrimshaw. Article decorated with sea shells.

Sculpture D'Appartement. Name given to large pairs and groups of figures which were made for French salons in the time of Louis XIV.

Serinette. See BIRD-ORGAN.

Sevigné Bow. Brooch in the shape of a bow, popular in the 18th century.

Shagreen. Kind of untanned leather with rough granular surface made from the skin of a horse, ass, shark, seal, etc., and frequently dyed green.

Shagreen box

Snuff Box. Snuff container made in a wide variety of forms and materials. From the late 17th century onwards.

Solitaire. Both a game introduced in the 18th century and a tea set for one person.

Spice Box. Early 17th-century casket.

Standish. Inkstand on plate on four feet with sometimes a drawer beneath for housing quills.

Snuff Boxes

Stencilled Playing Card

Typical Tazza

Staunton Chess-men. Popular set of chess-men designed by the Hon. Howard Staunton, son of the Earl of Carlisle, and patented by him in 1849.

Stencilled Playing Cards. Most cards were stencilled up to about 1830.

Stencilling. The application of paint to a surface through a water-proof paper in which the required pattern has been cut out.

Swagger-sticks. Short canes popular in the 18th and early 19th century, bearing loops so that they could be hung from the wrist.

Tambour. Circular frame consisting of one hoop fitting closely over another and over which material is stretched for embroidery.

Tantalus. Spirit stand containing decanters which can only be removed when the bar enclosing them is unlocked.

Taperstick. Small version of the candlestick for holding a sealing taper. Late 17th century onwards.

Tappit Hen. Scottish pewter measure.

Tassies. Glass or paste impressions worn as jewellery. Named after James Tassie, who made many of them from the 1760s.

Taws. Small earthenware or stoneware balls used in the game of carpet bowls. Also Scottish term for marbles.

Tazza. Shallow ornamental bowl, mounted on a base.

Terrestrial Globe. Subject to many changes in style since the famous example by Martin Behaim in 1492, the globe was a favoured piece of furniture in 18th-century libraries.

Ting. Chinese incense burner standing on three feet.

Toddy-lifter. Pipette for transferring hot toddy from bowl to glass. Early 19th century.

Terrestrial Globe

Toy Theatre

Tole-peinte. A Jardinière—container for flowers.

Tombac. White alloy of copper used in Germany in the 18th century for making snuff boxes, etc.

Toy Theatres. Now principally objects of pleasure for children, these theatres enjoyed a considerable adult craze from the 1830s to the 1870s.

Toys. 19th-century name for small objects such as scent bottles, étuis, etc.

Transformation. See TRANSPARENCIES.

Transformation Playing Cards. Cards in which the suit signs were adapted to form familiar topical or personal pictures. From the early 19th century.

178

Transparencies. Coloured prints juggled with overlays and held up to a strong light to render various pictorial transformations. Pin-prick pictures were also a great favourite with the Victorians. Prick holes were made in prints and held to the light; sometimes different coloured papers were applied to render effect of sunlight or moonlight, etc.

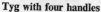

Tyg with four handles   **Examples of Vinaigrettes**

Treasury Inkstand. Having a double lid and four compartments for writing accessories, mounted on four feet.

Tric-trac. A game resembling backgammon.

Tulip (Pear). Pewter tankard with bulbous body.

Turlutaine. See BIRD-ORGAN.

Tutenag. See PAKTONG.

Tyg. Beaker, often with several handles.

Vinaigrette. Small ornamental bottle holding aromatic salts, etc. A smelling bottle.

Valentines. Card sent to a person of the opposite sex. Came into considerable vogue in the 1840s. Name derived from St Valentine, martyred by Claudius II for his protection of the Christians.

179

Wager Cup. Double cup in shape of skirted woman: intended to be drained without spilling from either cup.

Wassail Bowl. Two-handled loving cup.

Wax-flower Modelling. Wax flower arrangements under glass were much favoured by the Victorians.

Waxjack. Frame for coil of sealing wax taper. Mid-18th century onwards.

Wedge and Ball Thumbpiece

Wager Cup

Wedge Thumbpiece. Extension of a lid, frequently found on flagons and tankards. Also Wedge and Ball Thumbpiece.

Whistle Tankard. Tankards with blowhole, or small hole pierced in the castings or hollow members. The fable grew up that the hole was intended to be blown through to 'whistle' up' another drink, when in fact its purpose was to allow for expansion in soldering.

Witch Bottles. Stoneware bottles filled with oddities and used as charms.

PART FIVE

Furniture

Acanthus. A conventionalised leaf originating in classical architecture, and much used for decoration on furniture, silver, carpets, etc., in the 18th and (rarely) 17th century.

Acorn Clock. An American shelf clock made in New England in the first half of the 19th century, shaped roughly like an acorn.

Act of Parliament Clock. A term frequently but incorrectly applied to large, dialled, unglazed wall clocks. The term arose from a short-lived Act introduced by William Pitt in 1797, imposing a tax on all timepieces. Such large clocks were hung in taverns for the use of customers who had sold their own watches to avoid the tax.

Adze Surfaced Woods. A treatment applied to wood used in the construction of some medieval and Tudor chests. The adze was a hatchet-like tool which left ridges and hollows on the wood's surface.

Acanthus decoration

Act of Parliament Clock

Ambry. Enclosed compartment or recess in a wall or in a piece of furniture. Also referred to as aumbry and almery.

Amorini. Cupids; a motif frequently used on Restoration furniture and again in the late 18th century.

Andirons. Iron fire dogs dating back to Roman times. The earliest extant examples are of the 15th century.

Types of Andirons

Anthemion decoration

Andrea del Sarto Chair. Early 16th-century Tuscany chair; semi-circular with thin strip of wood supported on balusters acting as both back and arms.

Anglo-Japanese Design. A vogue current in the 19th century, satirised by W. S. Gilbert in *The Mikado*, inspired by examples of Japanese craftsmanship at the International Exhibitions in London and Paris in the 1860s.

Anthemion. An ornament of Greek derivation in radiating plant forms, sometimes known as the honeysuckle motif. Much used by Adam and his successors of the Regency period.

Aogai. A form of Japanese lacquer work making use of mother-of-pearl as an inlay.

Applied Ornament. Ornament individually carved and afterwards applied to furniture and silver.

182

Appliqué. Brass decorations on clock cases; also on wall lights.

Apron. Wooden apron extending downwards from the lower edge of a member (e.g. shaped lower edge on front of certain boarded chests, or below drawers of dressers); also below seating of close chair.

Apron Piece. An ornamental member, carved or shaped, beneath the rail of a chair or settee; also found below the frieze of cabinet stands and dressers.

Arabesques. An inlaid, painted or carved adornment of flat surfaces, composed of leaves, scrolls or animal forms, exemplified in the floral and 'seaweed' marquetry decoration of c. 1700 and later in the Adam period.

Arcaded Decoration. A series of arches on colonnettes or pillars (c. 1610–70), carved on chests, dressers and apron pieces.

Arcaded decoration

Architectural Clock

Architectural Clock. A clock, the hood or top of which has a classical pediment with or without supporting columns. The term is also applied where the same principle is found in the design of cabinets and wall mirrors.

Typical Ark

Astragal moulding

Ark. A chest with coped or gabled lid.

Armada Chest. Strong boxes in use before the invention of the modern safe in the 19th century. Supposed to be survivals from wrecked Spanish ships of the Armada, but in the main manufactured in Germany and imported in the 17th and 18th centuries.

Armadio. Companion piece to the cassone in 14th-century Italy (q.v.); a large cupboard (ARMOIRE), usually about four feet high and sometimes decorated in the Gothic manner.

Arming Chests. Chests used to house armour and weapons.

Armoire. French term for wardrobe, originating in the 17th century.

Articulated. Term used for hinged or swinging brass candle branch.

Astragal. A small, plain, semi-circular moulding; a term also used for the glazing bars of case furniture. Dating from c. 1750.

Athenienne. Candelabrum composed of urn supported on classical tripod, by J. H. Eberts, editor of the *Monument de Costume*, and derived from a French painting showing a priestess burning incense at a tripod of the same type, *La Vertueuse Athenienne*. Mounts of patinated bronze, ormolu or giltwood.

184

Atlanta. A sculptured male figure, or half figure, used as a support in place of a column. Found in classical architecture and adopted in the 17th and 18th centuries in the decoration of oak furniture.

Bachelor's Chest. A narrow chest of drawers of the Queen Anne period with a folding top for writing, probably used in bedrooms.

Example of Atlanta. Bachelor's Chest. Ball and Claw Foot; Ball Foot

Back Stool. A term used in the 17th and 18th centuries to describe an upholstered single chair. Derived from the Elizabethan period when stools were backed for greater comfort when dining.

Bail Handles. An American term for a half-loop metal handle, as in brass, secured by metal bolts. First used in America about 1700, it became the most popular form of drawer handle between 1720 and 1780.

Ball and Claw Foot. Terminal to a cabriole leg, representing a dragon's claw holding a ball. Popular in England in the Georgian period; also in America.

185

Balloon Back Chair.   Balloon Clock.   Example of Baluster

Ball Foot. Round terminal to late 17th-century cabinet and table legs.

Balloon Back Chair. An early Victorian chair with broad shoulder board derived from the Grecian and scrolled in the Louis XIV style.

Balloon Clock. A clock with a waisted cabinet popular towards the end of the 18th and beginning of the 19th centuries.

Baluster. A turned column, variously shaped, the vase-shape being the most familiar in the early 17th century.

Bamboo Turning. Furniture made from a soft wood in the late 18th century, simulating natural bamboo, usually painted or japanned.

Banding. A decorative inlaid border in contrasting wood or woods.

Banister-back Chair. A chair with a tall back consisting of splats of split-banister form popular in America in the early 19th century; usually of maple and frequently ebonised.

Banjo Clock. An American wall clock shaped roughly like a banjo. Barometer cases are frequently banjo-shaped.

Bantam Work. Incised lacquer imported from the Dutch East India Company in Java.

186

Bamboo Turning   **Banister-back Chair**   **Banjo Clock**

Bargueño. Sometimes called Vargueño. Spanish cabinet with fall-front enclosing drawers.

Barley Sugar. See TWIST TURNING.

Barley-turned. Resembling barley sugar. See TWIST TURNING.

Baroque. Decoration observed in late Stuart carving, and particularly in carved and gilt furniture of c. 1725–50. A more extravagant version of Renaissance decoration, much employed by Kent and his contemporaries.

Bas Relief. Low relief, carving or modelling in which figures project less than half of their true proportions from the background.

Basin Stand. See WASHING STAND.

Bead and Reel. A decorative inlaid border, applied particularly to 'Nonesuch' chests (q.v.) in the 16th and 17th centuries.

Bead Moulding. An 18th-century moulding found on furniture and metal work, resembling a string of beads, sometimes composed of semi-circular sections.

187

Bead-work. Articles ranging from shallow baskets in the 17th century to caskets, looking-glass frames and, in the 17th, 18th and 19th centuries, purses, in which the application of coloured glass beads formed the decorative motif.

Bed-warmer. Covered metal pans, for the reception of hot charcoal, with long wooden handles; mostly made in brass, but a few examples survive in silver.

Bedstead. The most popular forms among collectors are the box or enclosed bedstead, and the truckle or trundle bedsteads with wheels at the base of the uprights.

Beehive Clock. A small shelf clock, made in Connecticut (c. 1859–60), so named from its resemblance to an early beehive.

Beer Wagon. See COASTER.

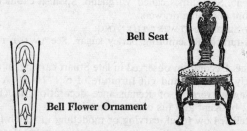

Bell Seat

Bell Flower Ornament

Bell Flower Ornament. A carved or inlaid pattern of flower beds wrought on the legs of tables and chairs, diminishing in size towards the base. An American term.

Bell Legs. A form of baluster leg with turned 'bell-like' top.

Bell Seat. Also known as the balloon seat. A rounded, bell-shaped seat of mid-18th-century origin often found in Philadelphia.

Types of Bellows   **Bended Back Chair**   **Typical Bergère**

Bellows. Contrivance of wood and leather for causing a draught artificially. Examples earlier than the 19th century are very rare, although they were manufactured from the 16th century onwards.

Bended Back Chair. Term given to early 18th-century walnut chairs with hooped backs and curved shaped splat designed for comfort.

Bent Back Chair. Variant of Spoon back.

Bentwood. Wood steamed and bent to form structural members of chairs, etc. First developed in Germany in the 19th century, and later widely employed in England.

Bergère. A winged armchair or couch with upholstered sides, popular in France in the mid- and late 18th century. Anglicised as Birjair or Burjair.

Bible Box. A box or chest of varying sizes intended to accommodate family bibles, but often used as a receptacle for general articles.

Bible Box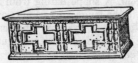

Bibliotheque Basse. A low cupboard with shelves for books with glass doors and, in some cases, grilles.

Bilbao. American wall mirror framed in coloured marble or marble and wood with scrolled headpiece and gilded mouldings in the Adam or Hepplewhite style. Believed to have originated in the Spanish seaport of Bilbao.

Bird's-eye Veneer. Often found in the wood of the sugar maple, the term arose from the pattern of small spots on the wood likened to birds' eyes.

Birdcage Support. A revolving platform on a tripod base.

Birdcage Support

Block-front chest of drawers

Blackamore Table. Table supported by negro's head in form of a caryatid, popular during Regency.

Blind Chinese Fret. A fret cut on the face of the wood only, not right through.

Blister. American term. A blister-like marking found in woods, particularly cedar, mahogany, pine, poplar and maple.

Block-front. A shape dating from the late 18th century and applied to the facing of various types of American furniture, notably chests of drawers. The term describes thick boards fronting drawers and cabinets so cut that the centre is concave and the ends convex.

Blowing Tube. A long metal tube which, blown through, produced a draught like the bellows which it preceded and with which it was also in contemporary use.

Boarded Chest. Primitive predecessor of the framed or joined chest.

Boat Bed. Empire style, in the shape of a gondola. American.

Bobbin-turned. Turned on a pole-lathe and applied to table legs particularly during the Commonwealth period; the shape resembled a bobbin.

Bolection Moulding. Ogee-shaped moulding projecting below edges of panels.

Bombé Form commode

Bonheur-du-Jour

Bombé Form. French term describing convex-shaped furniture, notably commodes; also applied to any curved or swelling shape.

Bonheur-du-Jour. Small writing table (c. 1700), usually on tall legs and sometimes adapted to hold toilet accessories.

Bonnet Top. American. Solid hood surmounting a piece of case furniture with a broken arch pediment façade.

Book Rest. A stand of square or rectangular construction with cross bars, the upper bar supported by a strut adjusted on a grooved base. Used in Georgian libraries to support large books, and occasionally fitted into a table-top.

Boss. An added section, carved or turned, found on Jacobean furniture.

Boston Rocker. Popular American rocking chair, a version of the English Windsor Rocker.

Book Rest

Boston Rocker

Boulle (Buhl). Descriptive of decorative inlay in metals and tortoiseshell executed by André Charles Boulle (1642–1732). Later practised in England.

Bow Back. See WINDSOR CHAIR.

Bow-fronted. Convex fronted furniture, familiar in the designs of Sheraton, notably chests of drawers.

Box. Made in a variety of shapes and woods from medieval times for the storage of personal effects, toilet and writing materials, documents, etc. In Tudor and early Stuart period, square, of oak, carved, inlaid or painted, and sometimes mounted on stands. In the late 17th century, commonly of walnut, but also of parchment, tortoiseshell and stump-work (the latter particularly for cosmetic boxes); in the 18th century mahogany and satinwood were employed giving way, in the 19th century, to the more familiar work-table.

**Box Toilet
Mirror**

Brazier

Box Toilet Mirror. Mirror mounted on a box with drawers.

Boys and Crowns. Ornament or cresting (17th and early 18th century) carved on chairs and day beds. The motif is a crown supported by two flying or sprawling naked boys.

Bracket Foot. Supporting foot to case furniture attached directly to the underframing. Introduced c. 1690.

Branches. Description of 17th- to 18th-century chandeliers.

Bras-de-Lumière. See WALL LIGHTS.

Brazier. Large flat pan for holding burning charcoal, used for heating dishes; precursor of spirit lamps and chafing stands.

Break-front Bookcase. Bookcase, popular in the mid-18th century, in which the central section projects beyond the side sections or wings.

Breakfast Table. Small, four-legged table with hinged flaps

Breakfast Table

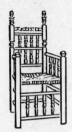

Brewster Chair

Buffet

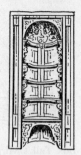

Broken Pediment

which may be extended on brackets, illustrated by Chippendale in 1762.

Brewster Chair. American term for early 17th-century Dutch type armchair made of turned posts and spindles. One was said originally to have been brought to America by William Brewster in the Mayflower.

Broken Pediment. An architectural motif borrowed by Georgian cabinet makers in the construction of bureaux, bookcases and similar pieces.

Bronzes d'Ameublement. Lacquered, patinated or gilt-bronze furniture ornaments.

Brushing Slide. Sliding shelf above the top drawer of certain commodes and chests of drawers of the second half of the 18th century.

Buffet. Sideboard, recessed cupboard for china, etc.

Buffet Chair. Precursor of the Windsor Chair.

Buhl. See BOULLE.

Bulb. Swollen member of turned support on Elizabethan and Jacobean furniture, often with carved Ionic capital above, and with moulding of 'cup and cover' form. Flemish origin.

Bun Foot. A flattened ball foot, introduced in the late 17th century.

Bureau Bookcase

Example of Bulb

Bureau. Writing desk with drawers.
Bureau Bookcase. A combined bookcase and slope front desk, the shelves above enclosed by doors, sometimes glazed. Mid-18th century.
Bureau à Cylindre. Rolltop desk.
Bureau-de-dame. A small bureau.
Bureau-toilette. Combined toilet and writing table, sometimes known as bureau-de-dame.
Burgomaster Chair. Circular chair of Dutch origin; sometimes called a roundabout chair and allied to corner chair.
Busse Chests. Buscarls' or seamen's chests.
Butler's Tray. A tray with folding legs or X-shaped stand in use in the 18th century.

Butler's Tray

Butterfly Table

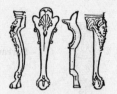

Types of Cabriole Legs

Butterfly Table. Drop-leaf table with supports in the shape of butterfly wings. American.

Cabinet-maker. A term for the new race of craftsmen who arose as the demand came for greater refinement in the decoration and construction of furniture, previously the exclusive reserve of the joiner. The technique of veneering, introduced at the return from the Continent of Charles II and which necessitated a flush surface not possible with the joiner's custom of utilising the panel and frame construction, gave special impetus to this evolution.

Cabochon. A motif in the form of an oval and usually convex gem, bordered by ornamental carving, found on the knees of cabriole legs, c. 1740.

Cabriole Leg. Curved outwards at the knee and inwards at the

Camel Back Sofa

foot; in general use c. 1700–50. The name cabriole originally denoted a small armchair.

Calendar Clock. A clock showing, in addition to the hours of the day, the passage of days, months and years.

Camel Back Sofa. Colloquial term for a sofa with a top shaped somewhat like a camel or dromedary.

Candelabrum

Candle Stand

Cane Chair

Camel Stool. A folding travelling stool.

Canapé. French word for a sofa. From the Louis XV period.

Candelabrum(a). Large, usually branched candlestick.

Candle Stand. A portable stand for a candlestick, candelabrum or lamp.

Cane Chair. Popular introduction in the reign of Charles II for its cheapness, lightness and durability. Adopted in America c. 1690 in the form of William and Mary tall-back chairs. Later revived in England in the classical style.

Canted. A bevelled, chamfered, or obliquely faced surface.

Canterbury. A music-stand with partitions for music-books;

Canterbury   **Caqueteuse Chair**   **Capstan Table**

the name was also applied in the 18th century to a plate and cutlery stand designed for supper parties.

Capstan Table. Known also as a Drum Table. Circular table with a deep frieze for drawers supported on a tripod or pedestal with three-sided solid base.

Caqueteuse. Known as a 'conversational' chair, introduced into Scotland from France in the late 16th century. The chair had a triangular seat, narrow back and spreading arms.

Carcase. The body of a piece of furniture on which thin veneer is applied.

Card-cut. Ornament carved in low relief in lattice form, featured in 'Chinese' furniture of Chippendale period.

Carlton House Writing Table. 'D' shaped writing table with drawers situated at the flat side; also in a border at the top, which is crested by a brass gallery. The name derives from the tradition that this type of table was first supplied to the Prince of Wales, later George IV, for Carlton House. Usually of mahogany but sometimes of satinwood.

Carolean. Strictly, term applicable exclusively to objects made in the reign of Charles I.

Cartonnier. Piece of furniture designed to hold paper; sometimes called a 'serre-papier'.

Cartouche. Scroll ornament with rolled-up ends bearing arms, a monogram or an inscription frequently found on apron pieces or as the centre of cabinet pediments. Variant of the escutcheon.

Carver Chair. Named after John Carver, first governor of the Plymouth colony, who is said to have taken an example to America in the Mayflower. An early 17th-century 'Dutch' type armchair constructed of turned posts and spindles.

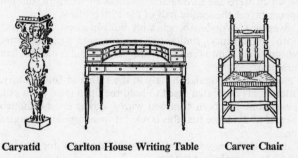

Caryatid   **Carlton House Writing Table**   **Carver Chair**

Caryatid. A support in the form of a sculptured female figure found on chest and cupboard fronts in the early 17th century, which revived in popularity towards the end of the 18th century.

Casket. Caskets made in Sicily in the 13th and 14th centuries may still be found; constructed of ivory, with brass mounts, they have been attributed to Arabic workmanship. The most common German manufactured casket dates from the second half of the 16th century. Fine coffers, the most conspicuous

199

Type of Casket

Cassone chest

of which were the incomparable works of Bickford, did not appear before the second half of the 17th century.

Cassapanca. Wooden bench with built-in chest under seat (15th–16th century), similar to a cassone, with back and arms, but surviving it into the 17th century as a popular piece of hall furniture.

Cassone. Chest popular in Italy in the 15th and 16th century. Often richly decorated, used to hold the linen (also to sit on), the cassone has been confused with a dower chest although there is no evidence that this is what it was originally intended for.

Cat. A three-legged stand (mid-18th century) for holding plates to warm before the fire.

Example of a Cat

Cavetto moulding

Causeuse, or 'love-seat'

Causeuse. Colloquially known as a 'love-seat'; a large chair or small sofa to accommodate two persons.

Cavetto. Concave moulding used on cornices of furniture, particularly in the period mid-17th to early 18th century.

Ceiler. Fabric head of medieval 'hangyd' bed, later replaced by the wooden headboard and, in turn, by the wooden roof or tester.

Cellaret. Case or sideboard with compartments for holding wine, etc.

Chaise à la Dauphine. 1755–60. Name given to a folding seat of this period. The subsequent addition of a low back to the webbed seats was occasioned by the Dauphine's complaint that they caused injury to her back. The chair thus modified was known as a 'perroquet'.

Chaise-longue. Low, extended seat to support sitter's legs, with back and arm rests.

Cellaret   **Chaise-longue**

Chaise Perspective. Walnut chair, upholstered and ornamented with carvings of colonnades and arcades represented in perspective. Louis XVI period.

Chamfered. A smoothed-off or bevelled edge.

Chandelier. Ornamental branched hanging support for a number of candles or lights.

Chandelier

Channelling. Parallel grooving or fluting on stiles of oak furniture; also on backs of Hepplewhite chairs.

Chasing. Ornamental engraving on metal, especially associated with ormolu mountings and mahogany secretaires in the Empire style.

Chateau-gendarme Finial. Finials shaped like the top section of a helmet.

Cheese Warmers. Shallow, rectangular trays with rounded corners and turned wooden handles, c. 1725–50.

Chequer. Inlay of light and dark woods forming a pattern like a chess board, much used during the 16th and 17th centuries.

Chest-on-chest. See TALLBOY.

Chesterfield. Sofa with stuffed, and sometimes cushioned, seat back and ends. Named after an Earl of Chesterfield.

Cheval Glass. Full-length toilet mirror, framed and supported on four legs.

Cheval Screen. As cheval glass with screen in place of mirror.

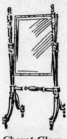

Cheval Glass

Cheval Screen

Cheveret. Secretaire of particularly light and elegant construction, often taking the form of a small table with tapering legs and a drawer supporting a little portable stand, with a handle and shelves to accommodate books. Late 18th century.

Chevron. A moulding or inlay of zig-zag shape.

Chiffonier. French. A tall chest of drawers. Introduced into England in the Regency period, the chiffonier seems to have been translated into a movable low cupboard with top forming sideboard. This fact has given rise to confusion with the French 'chiffonire' which was, similarly, a small piece of furniture—a small set of drawers on legs, with shelves for books.

Cheveret

Chimney Glass. Wide mirror situated above the chimney-piece, usually in three plates, a large central plate flanked by two smaller ones.

China Stand. Ornamental display stand for china or flowers, introduced at the end of the 17th century and subsequently taking a wide variety of forms.

China Stand

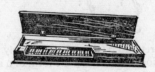

Clavichord

China Table. China or tea table, the top surface of which is surrounded by a gallery of lattice work with a Chinese motif.

Chinkinbori. Literally translated: sunk gold engraving. A Japanese lacquer-work technique.

Chinoiserie. Imitation of Chinese motifs in furniture, etc., fashionable in 18th and early 19th century.

Chip Carving. Crude shallow ornamentation on early (16th-century) chests executed with chisel and gouge.

Chipboard. Modern material made up of wood chips bonded under pressure with glues.

Clavichord. Small stringed musical instument which preceded the piano. See HARPSICHORD.

Claw Ball Foot. See BALL AND CLAW FOOT.

Clepsydra. A time-keeper motivated by water, running either into or out of it. Water clocks are among the earliest form known.

Close Stool (or Chair). Also referred to as a night stool. In various forms from a chair-shape to a rectangular box on legs, with a box top, generally intended for sanitary purposes.

Club Foot. Resembling head of club; the most common terminal of a cabriole leg (c. 1705 to late 18th century).

Close Stool	Clustered Columns	Type of Coaster

Cluster Supports. A series of legs supporting a table. Used by Chippendale.

Clustered Columns. A cluster of pillars adopted from the motif found in medieval architecture by exponents of the Gothic style in the mid-18th century.

Coaching Table. A folding table.

Coal Vase. Japanned container for coals used in the wealthier homes from the mid-19th century in place of scuttles.

Coaster. Also known as slider, decanter stand, and beer wagon. A receptacle for moving wine, beer or food on the dining table, made variously in mahogany, papier mâché and silver, fitted with small wheels or with baize-covered base.

Cobirons. Similar to andirons, but mostly plain in design with hooks for the accommodation of spits.

Cock Beading. Small, plain, semi-circular moulding applied to the edges of drawer fronts, 1730–1800.

Cobiron   Cock's Head Hinge   Coffer

Cock's Head Hinge. Twin-plate hinge, the finials of which are shaped like a cock's head. Frequently found on late 16th-century and early 17th-century woodwork, secured by hand wrought iron nails.

Coffer. Strong-box, like a chest, often covered in leather and banded with metalwork. Used for storing valuables.

Coffer Bach. Welsh Bible-box dating from the second half of the 18th century. Mostly of oak construction and sometimes lined with holly. Many 20th-century copies exist.

Coffin Stool. A term often misapplied to the stools used with refectory tables. A genuine coffin stool is much taller.

Coiffeuse. A dressing table of the Louis XVI period.

Collar. A decoration, generally of gilt or ormolu, on the top of turned sections of legs, much used in Louis XVI period.

Collector's Cabinet. A chest of small drawers, used for a collection of coins, butterflies, etc.

Comb-back Chair. Sometimes known as a 'stick chair', a forerunner of the bent, hoop-back Windsor chair, dating from the mid-18th century. The name derives from the comb-like appearance of the cresting rail and spindles.

Comb-back Chair **Connecticut Chest** **Console Table**

Commode. French term for chest of drawers, adopted in England to mean chests with serpentine fronts.

Concertina Framework. A form of hinging to be found on some 18th-century card and side tables, the top flaps being hinged and supported by the extension of two legs constructed on a jointed framework.

Conch Border. Shell pattern.

Confidante. An upholstered settee with additional seats set at an angle beyond the arms. Illustrated by Hepplewhite in his *Cabinet Maker's and Upholsterer's Guide*.

Connecticut Chest. American. Chest, sometimes with one or two drawers, ornamented with applied bosses and split spindles, with three front panels carved in low relief, a sunflower pattern on the central panel, tulips on the side panels.

Console Table. Wall table supported by two brackets; term also applied to side table surmounted by long mirror.

Constitution Mirror. American applied term for a Chippendale-style wall mirror decorated at the sides by leaves and flowers and with a scrolled-arch top and finial frequently in the shape of a bird. The origin of the name is obscure.

Convertible Chair. Table-chair or bench, c. 1680. Sometimes referred to as a monk's chair or bench; in the opinion of one authority at least, a misnomer.

Convex Frieze. Convex frieze or moulding customarily found on the straight cornices of late 17th-century chests-on-stands and tallboys.

Coquillage. Carved ornament in the shape of a shell; common in the mid-18th century on furniture in the French style (fr. *coquille*, a shellfish).

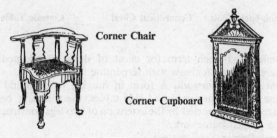

Corner Chair

Corner Cupboard

Corner Chair. Chair shaped conveniently to occupy a corner of a room, the legs being arranged one on each side, a third in the centre of the back and the fourth in the centre of the front. The chairback usually the same height as the armrest, the shape of the seat varying from a segment of a circle to rectangular. Known also as elbow or roundabout chairs in the 17th century.

Corner Cupboard. Shaped in a triangle to fit a corner, with a diagonal or curved front, usually fitted with shelving. Small hanging corner cupboards lacquered, or veneered in burr walnut, were very popular in the first half of the 18th century. Encoignures, standing corner cupboards, were in use in France in the reign of Louis XV.

Couch

Cornucopia. The horn of plenty, represented as a goat's horn overflowing with flowers, fruit and corn.

Couch. Piece of furniture like a sofa but with half back and head end only.

Counter. The term now familiar as a shop 'counter' originated as a piece of furniture for reckoning accounts with counters on a marked scale.

Court Cupboard. From the French word *court*: a short cupboard, in use in the 16th century, probably in the dining parlour; a three-tiered stand supported at back by plain posts, at the front by bulbous columns.

Courting Mirror. Traditional courting gift in New England in the 18th century; a small mirror bearing a crest on which is a painting or design.

Example of a Counter

Court Cupboard

Credence. Italian *credenza*. A term sometimes applied to a side-table in a church on which the Elements were placed before Consecration. In Italy, from the 15th century, used as a serving table, normally covered with linen, and often for the display of silver.

Creepers. Small irons, used in pairs, placed in the hearth between andirons, which they resembled in shape. 17th century.

Credence Table

Croft

Cresting Rail. Horizontal or top rail on the back of a chair variously decorated (17th and 18th century).

Crinoline Stretchers. Hooped stretchers, usually found on Windsor chairs.

Croft. Late 18th-century filing cabinet, small and portable with drawers and writing top. So called after its inventor.

Cromwellian. The term has earned currency in loose application to English furniture of an austere character, stemming supposedly from the Commonwealth period. In modern parlance a Cromwellian chair has a leather seat and back,

Cromwellian Chair

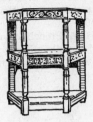

Type of Cup-board

ornamented with brass-headed tacks, on turned legs and occasionally spirally turned stretchers.

Cromwellian Clock. See LANTERN CLOCK.

Cross Banded (or Cross Grained). Decoration of a veneered surface in which a border of contrasting wood, cut across the grain, is applied to a piece of furniture.

Cross Garnet Hinge. Strap hinge in the shape of a 'T' laid on its side.

Cross Members. See STRETCHERS.

Cross Stretcher. Feature of late 17th and early 18th-century side tables and chairs; an 'X'-shaped stretcher, straight or curvilinear.

Cross-framed Legs. In which the front legs of the chair cross in serpentine fashion; typical of the Regency period and having a close affinity with the Egyptian style, c. 1805.

Crotch Veneer. See CURL VENEER.

Cup and Cover Supports. See BULB.

Cup-board. The cupboard as we know it did not come into existence until the end of the Tudor period. The original cupboard was a table or shelf for the display of family plate, sections of which in many instances were enclosed. Food cupboards, introduced c. 1500, had pierced doors for ventilation. See also LIVERY CUPBOARD.

211

Cupid's Bow Cresting. Characteristically formed the top rail of a chair or chairback settee of the Chippendale period, c. 1750.

Curfew. French *couvre-feu*. A quarter-sphere metal cover, with handle affixed, sometimes of brass or copper, used to cover an unattended fire and to keep it alight during the night.

Curfew

Cylinder-top Desk

Curl Veneer. Cut from just below the fork in a tree, revealing the full beauty of the grain, used by cabinet-makers to form patterns resembling an ostrich plume.

Cushion Frieze. Convex feature of cornice common in late 17th-century case furniture.

Cusps. Motif employed in mid-18th-century 'Gothic' furniture; the apexes between small arcs in 'Gothic' tracery.

Cwp Tridarn. Welsh. Three-tiered, enclosed cupboard resembling the press cupboard. A two-tiered version is known as a cwp deuddarn.

Cylinder-top Desk. Writing table with drawers and writing accessories closed by means of a curved panel fastened with a lock. According to certain authorities the cylinder-top desk differs from the roll-top desk in that the curved panel is in one piece and not slatted.

Cyma Recta. Moulding composed of two curves, the upper of concave form. Conversely, the cyma reversa is a moulding composed of two curves, the lower of concave form.

D-end Table. A table with two 'D'-shaped ends and one or two leaves.

Dangle-spit. A non-mechanical type of spit for roasting meat over a fire.

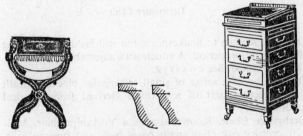

Dantesque Chair. Cyma Recta, Cyma Reversa.
Davenport writing table

Dantesque Chair. 15th-century chair with 'X'-shaped legs which might be folded for travelling. A few of wood, mostly of metal rods. A back was added to the seat in the 16th century. Another version followed known as the Savonarola chair.

Davenport. (1) Small ornamental writing table with drawers and hinged writing slab. (2) American large sofa.

Daventry. A small chest of drawers with a sloping top for writing; named after the inventor.

Day of the Month Clock. Clock which indicates the passing days of the month but which has to be adjusted by hand for short months, as distinct from the Perpetual Calendar Clock which is mechanically self-adjusting.

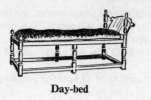

Day-bed

Derbyshire Chair

Day-bed. Known to Shakespeare but still fashionable during the Restoration period. A couch with adjustable back rest.

Decanter Stand. See COASTER.

Dentil. One of a series of small rectangular blocks beneath the projecting part of a cornice. Derived from classical architecture.

Derbyshire Chair. Known also as a Yorkshire chair. Mid-17th-century oak chair, with panel back and hooped rails, ornamented with carving, or an arcaded open back.

Derbyshire Desk. Carved oak writing-box.

Derbyshire Marble. Used without notable success by the early Victorians in furniture construction.

Desk Box. Rectangular box, with sloping lid, for the accommodation of books or writing materials. Much used as a Bible box (q.v.) in America.

Diaper. Ornamental design of diamond pattern used mostly for border decoration.

Dipped Seat. A variant of a saddle-back chair, the seat shaped in wood or covered with upholstery.

Directoire Style. While strictly named in reference to the Directoire period (1795–9), the term is loosely applied to French furniture and decoration in the last decade of the 18th century.

214

Desk Box   Dolphin motif

Dish-top Table. Table with upward curved rim, sometimes rectangular and supported on four legs, sometimes pedestal tables. Mid-18th century.

Display Cabinet. A glass-fronted cupboard with shelves for the display of china, etc.

Distressed. A trade term for furniture which is badly worn.

Document Draw. A thin narrow drawer in a desk for important papers.

Dole Cupboard. Used in churches and other institutions in the 16th century for the charitable distribution of bread, etc. Usually an open-shelved hanging cupboard.

Dolphin. The head and body of the dolphin was employed as a motif for the decoration of furniture in the mid-18th century. The head alone sometimes formed the foot of a chair or stool.

Door Furniture. Finger plates, escutcheons, and door handles. Executed by Robert Adam in ormolu and by Wedgwood in pottery. Later became a specialist manufacture.

Double Chest. See TALLBOY.

Double Rope Twist. See TWIST TURNING.

Double-scroll Handle. 'S'-shaped handle.

Dovetail Hinge. Butterfly hinge, with junction of the leaves, in the shape of dovetails, at the narrow section.

Dowel Pin. Round, headless wooden peg used to join sections of timber in the oak period.

215

Dower Chest. Chest for the storing of a bride-to-be's trousseau or household linen.

Drake Foot. See DUCK FOOT.

Draw Table. In general use in the late 16th century and throughout the Stuart period; a table capable of extension by the drawing out of leaves at either end. Originally known as a 'Drawinge table'.

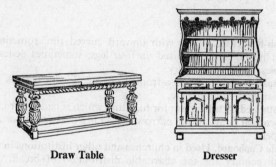

Draw Table   **Dresser**

Dresser. Kitchen sideboard with shelves for dishes, etc. In America the name is applied to a bedroom chest of drawers or dressing table.

Dressing Box. Toilet box fitted with compartments and a looking glass. In use in the Elizabethan age; much elaborated and decorated in the late 17th century when they were probably en suite with a dressing table.

Drop Handle. Known also as a tear drop or pear drop handle; a brass pendant handle hung from brass plate attached to drawer with pins. From about 1690 to 1720.

Drop-in Seat. Removable upholstered chair seat, first introduced about 1710.

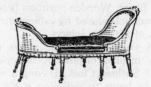

Drop Handles   **Duchesse**

Drop-leaf. Table with one or two hinged leaves, raised by extending swinging legs or supports. Examples include Gate-leg, Pembroke, etc.

Drum Top Table. See CAPSTAN TABLE.

Duchesse. A combination of two bergères linked by a stool, forming a type of chaise-longue.

Duck Foot. Also known as drake foot and web foot, but not to be confused with pad foot. Colloquial American term for a three-toed club foot found in Delaware Valley furniture.

Dug-out Chest or Trunk. Primitive form of chest, the interior gouged from a solid trunk. Of considerable antiquity, but reproduced at later periods.

Dumb Waiter. Three circular trays, increasing in size towards the bottom, supported on a shaft with tripod base. Early 18th century.

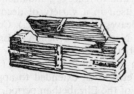

Dug-out Chest   **Dumb Waiter**

Dust Board. Wooden partition between drawers in a chest of drawers, introduced by cabinet-makers and not found in the work of the early joiners.

Dutch Oven. Open-fronted oven, made of sheet iron, brass and sometimes of pottery, for cooking before a fire.

Dutch Striking Clock. Having a mechanism which provides for the hours to strike on a big bell, the half-hours on a smaller, higher-toned bell.

Eagle's Head Cresting. Popular furniture ornament which took the place of the phoenix, used since the mid-18th century. Representation of the American national symbol—the American bald eagle with wings outstretched.

Ébéniste. French word for a cabinet-maker.

Echinus Moulding. The convex moulding next below the upper member of the capital of a column.

Egg and Tongue motif

Ecran à Pupitre. Literally 'screen desk'. See SCREEN TABLE.

Egg Motif Ornamentation. Ornamentation used in the 16th, 17th and 18th centuries, in which ovolo (egg) shapes alternated with other motifs—e.g. egg and dart border (alternating ovolos and arrow heads), egg and tongue, egg and anchor.

Egyptian Taste. Manifested itself in a variety of decorative motifs (sphinx heads, lotus leaves, lion heads, etc.). Current in France and England after Napoleon's invasion of Egypt.

Elbow Chair. See CORNER CHAIR.

Elizabethan. Objects made in the reign of Elizabeth I (1558–1603) are designated thus. Term often extended to apply to later pieces made in the style of the Elizabethan period.

Empire Style. Style current in France during period of

Napoleon's 1st Empire. The 2nd Empire, which also gave its name to a style of furniture, dates from the mid-19th century.

En Arbelette. A double curved shape, as employed in the construction of early bows (weapons).

Encoignures. See CORNER CUPBOARD.

End Boards. Solid boards carved in profile forming supports for Gothic stools or chests. In use up to the mid-16th century and afterwards, when they assumed a more elaborate form.

Endive Marquetry. See SEAWEED.

Typical Escutcheons

Espagnolette decoration

Entrelac-de-Rubans. See RIBBAND-BACK CHAIR.

Envelope Card Table. Table for the playing of cards, opening up by the raising of four lid sections shaped like envelope flaps.

Eolith. Flint, shaped by nature, used by early man as an implement or weapon.

Escritoire. Writing desk with drawers for stationery. See SCRUTOIRE.

Escutcheon. Pivoted key-hole cover.

Espagnolette. Female head with large stiff lace collar worn in 17th-century Spain, popularised by the engravings of Gillot and Watteau. Frequently used as a mounted decoration for furniture in the early 18th century.

Etagère. Small side table with shelves or trays set above each other. See WHAT NOT.

Ewery Cupboard. Early name for wash-stand; oak cupboard with a ewer and wash basin for washing and enclosed portion for towels and soap.

F Beneath a Crown. Crowned F is the mark of the Château de Fontainebleau.

Etagère   Farthingale Chair   Fauteuil

Fall Front. A fall front cabinet is a writing cabinet with small drawers, sometimes furnished with a stand for placing on a table or desk top. Fashionable in England in the late 17th century, and earlier in Italy and Spain.

Fall Slope. The flap of a bureau which opens outwards.

Falling Table. See DROP LEAF TABLE.

Fan Pattern. Fan motif introduced in chairbacks; also in carving, and inlay or painted decoration.

Fan-back Chair. See WINDSOR CHAIR.

Fancy Chair. American term covering a variety of occasional chairs, painted and with a cane seat.

Farthingale Chair. Introduced in the reign of James I and designed to accommodate a sitter wearing a hooped (or farthingale) dress. Armless, with a wide seat, usually upholstered in Turkey work or velvet.

Fauteuil. French armchair, the sides of which are not upholstered.

Feather Banding. See HERRINGBONE.

Federal Style. Descriptive of American furniture made during the early years of the Republic (1785–1830). Deriving from Hepplewhite, Sheraton, Directoire and early French Empire styles.

Figure of Eight Back Chair

'Fiddle' Figured Wood. Wood containing little streaks, as found on the back of fiddles.

Fielded Panels. Raised panel with bevelled edges, employed on 17th-century drawer and oak dresser fronts, etc.

Figure. The natural pattern in wood which cabinet-makers exploited to considerable effect, particularly with the introduction of veneers.

Figure of Eight Back Chair. Shaped as the name suggests; popular in Venice in the 18th century.

Fillet. A narrow strip of wood used to serve as a support or to strengthen an angle formed by two surfaces.

Finial. Ornamental projection, taking several forms such as an acorn or antique vase with drapery, found on furniture. Also applicable to the goldsmiths' work in the shaping of sugar casters, coffee pots, etc., in a variety of decorative motifs.

Fire Dogs. See ANDIRONS

Fire Fork. Fore-runner of the poker; a wrought iron instrument for moving burning logs in a fireplace, often four feet or more in length so as to protect the user from the heat.

Fire Fork   Fireback   Example of Fluting

Fire Screen. Protection from the heat of the fire. Two main varieties were the pole screen, supported on an upright with tripod base, and the horse or cheval screen in which the panel is enclosed by two uprights on legs. Late 17th century.

Fireback. Frequently referred to as a reredos; a cast-iron shield often decorated, placed at the back of a fireplace to protect the wall from the heat of the fire. The best known are Sussex made, but many were also imported from Holland in the late 17th century.

Fish-tail. Fish-tail pattern carving on top rail of a banister back chair.

Flag Seat. American chair seats woven with rush-like materials are frequently so described.

Flambeau Finial. A finial turned to imitate a flame.

Flame Mouldings. Mouldings in the shape of a flame used on wall brackets.

Flanders Chest. Appears in many inventories as 'overseas work'. Chests in very popular demand in the 16th century, originally imported from Flanders. Versions, less ambitiously carved, were in use in the 17th century.

Flemish Scroll. Curving double scroll, sometimes employed on late 17th-century chairs on the front legs and forward stretchers.

Flower Stand. See CHINA STAND.

Folding Table

Fluting. Derived from classical motif used on columns; a system of concave channels worked in close formation, extensively on silver cups in the late 17th century, and frequently on furniture in the last quarter of the 18th century (e.g. fluted legs).

Folding Table. Appeared in inventories as early as the 14th century; a table with one fixed and one hinged lid which could be folded back to rest on the fixed lid.

Footman

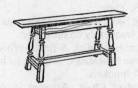

Example of a Form

Footman. Four-legged 'stool' made of brass or wrought iron, or both, often with cabriole legs and made to stand before a fire. Variation on the trivet.

Form. Long, backless seat with a number of supports from two upwards.

Forsets. Also known as fossets or fosselets. Smaller version of an earlier form of strong-box. By the 18th century had taken the form of cabinets as well as chests.

Four-poster. Bedstead with four posts supporting a canopy and with curtains which might be drawn to enclose the bed completely.

Franklin Clock. Type of shelf clock made in Plymouth, Connecticut (1825–30), with wooden movement.

Four-poster bed

'French' Chair

Furry Lion-paw Foot

'French' Chair. Post-Restoration, high backed, elaborately carved walnut arm chair, richly upholstered made en suite with stools. Examples exist of beech and gilt as well as walnut. Also, by the mid-18th century, mahogany chairs in the rococo style were referred to as 'French'.

French Scroll. See SCROLL FOOT.

Fretwork. Decorative application to galleries and friezes on tea-tables, chairs, etc., in mid-18th century. Often in the Chinese taste, also derivative from Gothic.

Frieze Drawers. Deriving from the architectural term, and used in connection with furniture to describe a band situated below a cornice.

Fundame. Japanese lacquer-work technique employing powdered gold worked to a matt surface.

Furry Lion-paw Foot. A lion-paw foot, either brass or wood, carved to resemble fur.

Example of Fretwork

 **Gadroon Border**

Gadroon Border. Patterned convex fluting used in the decoration of oak furniture in the late Elizabethan and Jacobean period and in mahogany in the mid-18th century; also for the decoration of silverware.

Galleried. A table, desk or stretcher surrounded with brass trellis.

Gaming Table. Made in a variety of forms, the earliest dating from the beginning of the 18th century. Constructed with folding top, essentially for card playing, with recesses at corners for candlesticks and wells for counters. Sometimes marked as a chess board.

Gardes du Vin. Brass-hooped cellarets by Hepplewhite, intended to occupy space beneath sideboard.

Gate-legged Table. Folding table with leaves supported on gate-shaped structure which may be swung back to allow the leaves to hang down.

Georgian Style. Applied to works of art made during the reign of the three Georges prior to the Regency.

Gaming Table

Gate-legged Table

Type of Girandole   **Glastonbury Chair**

Girandole. Name given to (a) carved gilt sconce of asymetrical design sometimes enclosing looking glass, (b) an American wall-clock designed by Lemuel Curtis, c. 1820.

Glastonbury Chair. Named from the original Abbot's chair at Glastonbury. 'Gothic' Tudor chair frequently found in the chancels of churches.

Glazing Bars. Used in elegant patterns on the glass doors of cabinets, bureau-bookcases and bookcases.

Gobelins, Manufacture Royale des. State-supported organisation founded in 1667, which supplied not only tapestries but a range of products covering the luxury arts and furniture.

Goose Neck Pediment. See BROKEN PEDIMENT.

Gothic. A 12th- to 15th-century style, revived by the 18th- and 19th-century imitators and widely applied to woodwork, metalwork, etc., as well as to architecture.

Gothic Credence. Form of buffet or cupboard with carved tracery and, in some cases, linen fold panels. Tudor period.

Gouge Work. Used widely in oak furniture in the 17th century. Scooped pattern made with semi-circular gouge.

Grandfather Chair. See WING CHAIR.

Grandfather Clock. Familiar name for a long case clock (q.v.).

227

Grecian Chair

Grandmother Clock. Long case clock (smaller than the Grand-father clock), no more than 6′ 6″ in height.

Grecian Chair. In fashion in the Regency period. Notable for its wide shoulder boards and 'sabre' front legs.

G.R.F. Mark of the Garde-Meuble Royal de Fontainebleau.

Grid-iron. Device formed of parallel bars which, placed over a fire, was used for cooking meat, etc.

Griffin. This legendary, half eagle half lion figure was much used as a decorative feature on Georgian furniture.

Grisaille. In which various tones of grey were employed for a painting. Frequently used as a decorative motif by Adam.

Gueridon. Originally took the form of a negro figure holding a tray. Named after a Moorish galley slave. Covers a variety

Type of Gueridon

Guilloche decoration

'H' Hinge

228

of small, usually circular pieces of furniture designed to support some form of light.

Guilloche. Border moulding incorporating interlaced ribbon enclosing foliate rosettes; used as a decorative pattern from the 16th to 18th century.

'H' Hinge. External hinge commonly used on cupboards in the 16th and 17th centuries, shaped like the letter 'H'.

Hadley Chest. Originating from Hadley, Massachusetts—a type of late 17th-century dower chest faced with incised carving of tulips, vines and leaves.

Hadley Chest   Harpsichord

Handkerchief Table. American term for a single leaf table which, closed, is in triangular shape, but when opened out forms a square.

Harlequin Pembroke Table. Table with a nest of drawers and pigeon holes which came up from within the table when the flap was raised.

Harpsichord. Like Clavichord (q.v.), a prototype of the grand piano.

Herring-bone Cross Banding. Veneer border comprised of two narrow strips of veneer laid diagonally to each other to form

Herring-bone Cross Banding

the shape of a herring bone or feather. Much used on walnut furniture of the late 17th and early 18th century.

Highboy. North American tall chest of drawers mounted on a commode or lowboy, having some likeness in principle to the English tallboy.

Hipping. Ornamental treatment of the knee of a cabriole leg in which the carving on the knee is extended to the seat rail. Found on the finer quality chairs and settees in the first half of the 18th century.

Hitchcock Chair. American version of the late 18th-century English painted or stencilled chair, named after Lambert Hitchcock, who made a large number of them between 1820 and 1850.

Hoof Foot. Terminal of late 17th-century cabriole leg, succeeded by the simpler Club Foot.

Hoop-backed Chair, Hoop-Shaped Back, Hoop-Shaped Seat. See WINDSOR CHAIR.

Horse Shoe Back Chair   **Highboy**   **Hitchcock Chair**

Type of Hutch

Ionic Column

Hope Chest. American term for dower chest. Such a chest was, however, frequently used to house other articles than a trousseau.

Horse Glass and Horse Screen. See CHEVAL GLASS and CHEVAL SCREEN.

Horse Shoe Back. American name for a hoop back Windsor chair.

Husks. Ornament derived from the husk of a wheat ear, used singly, sometimes pendant, or in festoons. Characteristic of the Adam and Hepplewhite period.

Hutch. Enclosed construction, sometimes on uprights, sometimes having more than one tier. The food hutch is composed of perforated panels.

'India' Wall Paper. Comprehensive term for paper hangings and similar articles made in the Far East and designed for the European market in the 18th century.

Indian Mask. Mask with plumed head-dress employed as a decorative motif on crestings, especially on mirrors at the end of the 17th century and beginning of the 18th.

Inlaid Furniture. Ornament applied to furniture in the shape of different coloured woods, bone, ivory, shell, etc., in a recessed ground. Popular on chair backs, chests, tables, etc., from the 16th century. Not to be confused with marquetry (q.v.).

Intarsia. See TARSIA.

Ionic Column. Architectural term also applied to furniture. The Ionic column is one of the three Greek orders characterised by two lateral volutes of the capital. Customarily

Joint Stool

Example of a Kas

employed as supports for Regency pier glasses and other furniture of that period.

Jacobean. Term strictly applicable to objects made in the reign of James I, and sometimes James II; often loosely ascribed to furniture styles in direct descent from the Elizabethan tradition.

Jambs. Side posts of door-way, window, etc. (e.g. stone jambs on Jacobean chimney-pieces).

Japanning. Decorative treatment of furniture woods in which a coating of whiting and size was applied, coats of coloured varnish being subsequently added to form the ground. The design was then painted on in gilding and in colours mixed with gum-arabic.

Jardinière. Ornamental pot or stand for the display of growing flowers.

Jewel Ornament. Raised ornament somewhat resembling a gem-stone, often combined with geometrically designed raised mouldings.

Joiners. Craftsmen ultimately displaced by the cabinet-makers about the time of the Restoration, when the demand arose for more elegant and complex furniture construction. From this time joiners turned, in the main, to the making of simpler furniture and house fittings.

Kettle Stand

Kidney Table

Joint Stool. Stool made of parts fitted by joiner as distinct from one of clumsier workmanship.

Jousting Chests. Name given to chests carved in high relief with hunting, jousting scenes, etc. Origin uncertain, but many 19th- and 20th-century 'copies' exist.

Kas. Large clothes cupboard with panelled doors, overhung cornice and, usually, ball-front feet. Made between 1675 and 1750 by the Dutch settlers in the Hudson and Delaware River valleys.

Kettle Stand. Also urn and tea-pot stand. Introduced with the custom of tea drinking in the late 17th century. Takes the form either of a small table with tripod or four-legged support, having a gallery or raised edge round the surface area, or a box-like piece of furniture opening at the side with slide for tea pot.

Kettle-tilter. Also known as an 'idle-back', 'lazy-back' or 'handy-maid'. Wrought iron contrivance which hung from a pot-hook or crane over the fire and supported a kettle, which might be tilted for use without soiling or burning the hand.

Key Pattern. Classical frieze ornament composed of lines placed at right-angles to one another, much used in the Kent period. (See WILLIAM KENT, Part 7.)

Kidney Table. The first design for the famous kidney-shaped table appeared in Sheraton's *Drawing Book*.

Knee-hole Table

Knife Cases

Knee-hole Table. Table fitted with drawers and arched apron-piece in centre. Walnut examples of the late 17th and early 18th-century periods could be used as dressing or writing tables.

Knife Case. Knife and other cutlery container in use in the dining room, from the 17th century onwards. Took the form either of a box with sloping top and convex front with interior divisions or, later, of a vase-shaped case designed to stand on the sideboard on pedestals, the top of which could be raised, the knives being arranged around a central stem.

Knopped. A knop is a swelling member on a shaft, pillar or stem of cup or goblet. Also applied to ormolu loop-handles.

Ladder-back Chair

Lancashire Chair

| Lancet Clock | Lantern | Lantern Clock |

Knotted Pine. Second best plank of pine with rough knots, earlier despised and consequently painted over, but latterly in fashion and much admired by collectors in its natural form.

Knulled. Descriptive of decoration consisting of short fluting of irregular outline used on silver and plate in the mid-18th century; and also for borders and for handles.

Knurl Foot, Knurl Toe. See SCROLL FOOT

Labelled Furniture. Furniture on which is found the cabinet-maker's printed label.

Lacche. Italian term applied to all painted furniture.

Ladder-back. Chair back of curved horizontal rails, frequently pierced, found in the late Stuart period and, in mahogany, in the mid-18th century.

Lambrequin. Short piece of hanging drapery, often copied in metal or woods, designed for decorative purposes.

Lamin Board. Similar to blockboard, but thinner strips.

Lancashire Chair. A heavy stick-back chair.

Lancet Clock. Bracket clock with pointed 'Gothic' top. Late 18th and early 19th century.

Lantern. Transparent case protecting flame of candle, etc.

Lantern Clock. Typically English style of wall clock developed from the beginning of the 17th century up to the mid-18th cen-

Library Steps   **Lighthouse Clock**   **Linen Press**

tury. The name is said to have been inspired by the shape of
ships' lanterns of the period. Sometimes erroneously referred
to as 'Cromwellian' clocks.

Lattice Ornament. Low relief motif particularly applied to the
arm supports and front legs of mahogany upholstered chairs,
c. 1760.

Lazy Susan. American version of the dumb waiter in use in the
early 19th century for condiments.

Lenticle. The glass panel of a long case clock enabling the
motion of the pendulum to be seen.

Lever Clock. Late 18th century, patented by Robert Barron;
lock consisting of a mechanism of fixed wards combined with
two pivoting or uplifting tumblers, held in position by a steel
spring. Precursor of the conventional lever lock.

Library Steps. In use in the mid-18th century in large houses.
Some were of fixed construction with hand rails, others could
be folded and concealed in chairs, stools, tables, etc.

Lighthouse Clock. American. Shelf or mantel clock designed by
Simon Willard (c. 1800) on the principle of the Eddystone
Rock Lighthouse.

236

Linenfold carving. Lion Mask and Lion-Paw Foot. Livery Cupboard

Linen Press. Frame structure with wooden screw and two boards for pressing linen. From the 17th century.

Linenfold Carving. Carved ornament of Flemish origin, resembling in form folded linen, found in the 15th century and later, and used as decoration on wall panels, chair backs, chests, etc.

Lion Mask. Carved decorative motif in the shape of a lion's head, found on the knees of many cabriole legs made during the second quarter of the 18th century and revived during the Regency period in brass for drawer handles.

Lion-Paw Foot. Carved ornament found on gilt armchairs of the late 17th century; popularly employed as terminals to cabriole legs on early 18th-century chairs and side tables. Reappeared as a frequent motif in the Regency period.

Livery Cupboard. 'Livery' was a term used to describe the ration of food and drink dispensed for the night and eaten in the bedchamber. Livery cupboards were no longer in use after the 1660s. See also CUP-BOARDS.

Lobby Chest. A kind of half chest of drawers adapted for use in a small lobby, etc.

Lobing. See under GADROON and KNULLING.

Lock Plate. See SCUTCHEON.

Long Case
(Grandfather) Clock

Lotus motif

Loo Table

Long Case Clock. Made in England from the 1660s, up to 7ft and more in height, with veneer, lacquer, marquetry and other decorations. Also called Grandfather Clock.

Long Table. See under REFECTORY TABLE.

Loo Table. Early Victorian circular table, often with a papier-mâché top. Loo was a card game played with 3 or 5 cards, with penalties paid to the pool.

Looking Glass. In the 16th and 17th centuries mirrors were framed in the same style as pictures. It was not until the 18th century that they commanded the attention of frame makers in the very individual sense evidenced most particularly by the rococo taste, the use of wood and pottery, and the engraved glass frames emanating from Venice.

Loopback Chair. American. Type of Windsor chair.

Lopers. Brass elbow-jointed stays or oak slides which pulled out from slots to support flap of bureau or chest of drawers (c. 1700 onwards).

Lotus. The 'water lily of the Nile'; much used as a motif for decoration in Egyptian-style furniture of the Regency period.

Love Seat. See CAUSEUSE.

Lowboy. Modern name for American derivative of the English flat-top dressing table with drawers (18th century); later evolved into a piece resembling the French commode. Known also as a dressing table, chamber table or low chest of drawers, the lowboy was frequently an accompaniment to the highboy (q.v.).

Lunettes. Decoration in the form of a half moon, carved on later oak furniture; also inlaid and painted in Adam period.

Lyre Back Sides or Support. Familiar design applied to chairs by Robert Adam in the late 18th century. Splat carved in the shape of a lyre with metal springs. The same motif was in use for end supports and sides of low tables.

Mannerist Style. A manifestation of the reaction in the second decade of the 16th century against the classical spirit of the Renaissance. This intellectual and anti-naturalistic style emanated from the French court at Fontainebleau and spread throughout Europe with numerous local variations.

Marlborough Leg. A square, straight tapered leg sometimes supported on a plinth; made by cabinet-makers in the second half of the 18th century. May have been so called as a compli-

Lowboy

Lunettes

Lyre Back Chair

**Martha Washington
Sewing Table and Chair**

ment to the Duke of Marlborough, to whom Ince and Mayhew dedicated their *Universal System of Household Furniture*.

Marquetry. Decoration of flat surface, as of furniture, by glueing together shaped pieces of wood, iron or other substances, so as to cover the whole.

Marriage Chest. See DOWER CHEST.

Martha Washington. Name given to a chair, mirror and sewing table found in America in the mid-18th century. The chair was highbacked, usually with serpentine cresting, and had a low, shallow, upholstered seat. Martha Washington is supposed to have used a chair of this type at Mount Vernon. The mirror was framed in walnut or mahogany and was also known as a 'Constitution'. The sewing table was in oval, box form with hinged top, similar to the late 18th-century English sewing table.

Mask Handles. See LION MASK.

Meander Ornament. Border ornament comprising a series of straight lines intersecting at right angles; also known as Greek fret or key pattern.

Melon Bulb. Colloquial term for swollen members of legs or posts of furniture.

Mendlesham Chair. Variety of Windsor chair first made by Daniel Day of Mendlesham, Suffolk. Some high quality examples have inlay decoration on backs.

Menuisier. French term roughly corresponding to carpenter or joiner, as opposed to *ébéniste*, a cabinet-maker.

Menuisiers Ébénistes, Corporation De. Identified by J.M.E. stamped on furniture made by member craftsmen of the guild.

Meuble À Hauteur D'Appui. General term to describe any low bookcase or cupboard, usually between three and four feet high.

Meuble D'Entre Deux. Term used in 18th-century France to describe cupboards or chest of drawers flanked on each side by a set of shelves.

Mirror Stand. Adjustable mirror mounted on a shaft and tripod base. Popular at the end of the 18th century.

Mitre. Joint in which line of junction bisects the angle (usually at right angle) between the two pieces, as in a picture frame.

Modillion. Projecting bracket under corona of cornice found on furniture designed in accordance with the classical architectural orders.

Mokume. Japanese lacquer work technique imitative of wood graining.

Monopodium. Classical form of support for tables. Fashionable during the Regency period when support was in shape of animal head and body with single leg and foot. Later versions were made in a simpler manner.

Mortise or Mortice. A cavity, usually rectangular, made to accept a tenon, which was held fast by a peg. Introduced in the 16th century, it has remained the joiner's principle joint.

Mortuary Chair. Mid-17th-century chair with scrolled back. In the centre of the rails was a carving of a bearded head, traditionally thought to be Charles I.

Mother-of-Pearl. Inlay of nacrous shell slices. The Americans also made considerable use of this type of inlay in the decoration of fancy chairs, tables, etc., in the early 19th century.

Moulding. A shaped member used to form edge on lid or cornice, or to frame panel.

Example of Muntin

Night-table

Nail-head Decoration

Mule Chest. Collectors' slang for chest with drawers, the implication being a hybrid.

Muntin. Upright connecting upper and lower stretchers of wooden framework.

Nail-head Decoration. Small carved squares with raised point, resembling nail-head, used in series as a form of decoration on furniture from the Middle Ages.

Name Chest. Colloquial term for chest bearing name of original owner carved in decorative style.

Necessaire (De Voyage). Container for various small tools used for toilet or household purposes, e.g. earpicks, tongue scrapers, snuffing spoons, scent bottles, scissors, ivory tablets, etc.

Needlework Cabinet. Cabinet fitted either with doors or fall front with embroidered satin pieces on sides.

Neo-classical. Classical revival manifested in decoration associated with Robert Adam.

Neo-Greek. Furniture of the early 19th-century classical revival. More frequently applied to the late Empire style of 1815–40.

New England Armchair. American version of the hoop-back Windsor, with the exception that the hoop embraces the arms as well as the back.

Night-table. Pot cupboard which succeeded the close stool or chair (q.v.) after 1750. Sometimes combined with a wash-stand.

Nonesuch Chest

Occasional Table

Nonesuch Chest. Chest dating from about the mid-16th century so called because the inlay design was of buildings similar in design to the Palace of Nonesuch built for Henry VIII at Cheam.

Nulling. Similar to gadrooning. See GADROON BORDER.

Occasional Table. Small table intended to serve a variety of purposes. First introduced in the latter half of the 17th century.

Ogee. Moulding, showing in section a double continuous curve, concave below passing into convex above.

Onion Foot. A variation of the Bun foot, but turned in the shape of an onion.

Ormolu. Gilded bronze used for mounts of furniture and other decorative metalwork, especially in 18th-century France. Many articles are made of, and decorated with, a cheaper imitation, including a gold-coloured alloy of copper, zinc and tin.

Ottoman. Cushioned seat without back or arms (frequently a box with a cushioned top).

Outscrolled Arm Support. A scroll used to support the arm of a chair.

Overmantel. Ornamental carving, looking glass or other fixed attachment over mantelpiece.

Overstuffed Seat. Padded chair seat in which upholstery is continued over seat tail and secured beneath.

Ovolo Moulding. Border ornament used in the 16th, late 18th and early 19th centuries. Small, usually repetitive, oval convex moulding.

Oxbow Front. American term for bow-like front, a form often employed by Boston and other New England cabinet-makers in the 18th century.

Oyster Veneer. Of Dutch origin, introduced into England in the late 17th century. Resembles oyster shells placed side by side; effect achieved by the laying down of strips of wood cut from small branches.

Pad Foot. Resembling small club foot, and used as a terminal to cabriole legs of chairs, settees and tables. From the early 18th century.

Palace Letters. Often found painted or branded on French furniture, with the inventory numbers.

Palladian Style. Architectural style so-called after 16th-century Italian architect, Palladio. William Kent and the Earl of Burlington encouraged its revival in the first half of the 18th century, when it was applied to furniture as well as buildings.

Palmette. Ornament of Greek derivation based on the branch of a date palm.

Panel. Sunk or raised compartment on the surface of a framework, usually rectangular. As distinct from 'panelling', which comprehends panel and framework.

Panelled Chests. Constructions of loose panels secured by a framework held together by mortice and tenon joints. Characterises joiners' as opposed to carpenters' furniture.

Papier-mâché. Fibrous pulp mixed with chalk and sand and shaped in boxwood moulds. By the late 18th century an improved composition of ground rags, glue, flour and water was used.

Parchment Pattern. Sometimes described as linenfold carving, the form being as the name suggests. Found in the late 15th and early 16th centuries, of Flemish origin.

Oyster Veneer

Examples of Pad Foot

Parquetry. Form of geometrical veneer, first used in England in the second half of the 17th century.

Partners' Desk. A double-sided desk.

Patera. Classical ornamental motif, based on saucer used in sacrificial libations. Much employed in the Adam period.

Patina. Incrustation, usually green, on the surface of old bronze; esteemed as ornament. Also applicable to the surface of woodwork after centuries of polish and usage.

Paw Feet. Terminal to cabriole leg in shape of lion's paw. Mid-18th century, found especially on pieces inspired by William Kent.

Pear-drop Mouldings. Repetitive design of inverted pear-shaped forms found below cornice of late 18th-century bookcases.

Péché Motel. Similar to a Duchesse (q.v.). Couch consisting of easy chair and stool. Illustrated in Chippendale's *Director* (3rd edition).

Pedestal Table. Table with round top, tripod base, and supported on a central pillar. The legs are cabriole with club or claw-and-ball feet.

Patera motif

Pedestal Table

Pediment. An architectural term, meaning triangular end to roof, applied to cabinets, bookcases, etc., in the 18th century.

Pegged Chest. Chest which can be taken apart for travelling or storing by removal of the securing pegs.

Pembroke Table. Table on four legs, with short hinged flaps which may be raised and supported on brackets.

Pendent Husks. Ornaments in shape of wheat ears used by architects and craftsmen during the Adam period.

Pennsylvania Dutch. German settlers in Pennsylvania whose production of furniture in soft woods, painted with floral patterns, resemble the early English and German peasant styles.

Pendent Husks

Pembroke Table

Perroquet. Mid-18th-century chair with low back and webbed seat.

Pie-crust Table. Table with round tilt-top on three cabriole legs, the surface having scalloped edge. Mid-18th century.

Pier Glasses. Tall, elaborately carved mirrors, usually in pairs, hung in spaces between windows. 18th century.

Pier Table. D-shaped or semi-eliptical tables often placed beneath pier glasses. Earlier examples of gesso, later with marble or veneered satinwood tops.

Pietre Dure. Italian semi-precious stones much used for table tops, altar frontals, etc., in the 16th century.

Pilaster. Column of rectangular section projecting from a wall. Architectural motif sometimes applied to furniture.

Pie-crust Table   **Pier Glass**   **Pier Table**

Pilgrim Furniture. Generally used to describe furniture made during the 17th century for the American Puritans.

Pillar and Claw Tripod. Three legs of cabriole form, with claws, dovetailed to the base of a turned pillar.

Pin Lock. Usually made in oak and opened by a wooden key.

Pin-hinge. Method of hinging found on 13th-century chests.

Pipe-rack. Dating from the 18th century, in candlestick form with circular pierced tray on stem, or as wall-rack.

Pilaster   **Pipe-racks**

Pipe-tray. Long, narrow wooden tray with partitions for 'church-warden' pipes. Georgian.

Planked Oak. Furniture made of solid board, with no panels.

Plaquette. Oblong or oval decorations, cast in lead, silver or bronze, applied to 15th-century household utensils. Collectors' pieces from the 16th century.

Plate Pail. Mahogany container with handle for carrying plates from kitchen to dining room.

Plate-warmer. Several varieties of wood or metal construction. Placed before the fire to heat plates preparatory to serving. 18th and 19th century.

Pipe-tray　　　　**Planked Oak Chest**

Plinth. Architectural term for the square base of a column. Often employed as a terminal on feet of cabinet furniture pieces.

Plum Pudding Mahogany. A wood that is patterned with small dots, resembling the plums in a pudding.

Pole Screen. Fire screen on upright supported on tripod base. Late 17th century.

Poppy-(Popey)-head. Decorative finial on bench (or desk-end), derived from medieval ecclesiastical wood work.

Portuguese Bulb. Turned chair leg in form of inverted pear. Late 17th century.

Pot Board. Lower shelf of court or livery cupboard.

Plate Pail

Pole Screen

Pot-hook. Wrought-iron device for suspending pot over fire. Also known as cottrall, jib-crook, hanger, tramelle, hake.

Pounce Pot or Box. See SAND-BOX.

Press or Press Cupboard. Clothes or linen cupboard.

Prie-dieu. Tall-backed chair with low seat intended for prayer.

Purdonium. Metal-lined coal box with padded seat, thought to have been invented by a man called Purdo.

Puritan Furniture. Name applied to simple utility American furniture of the 17th century. See PILGRIM FURNITURE.

Press Cupboard

Prie-dieu

249

Quartetto Tables

Quartetto Tables. Nests of four tables.

Rabbet. Lengthways groove on piece of wood to which edge of board can be fitted.

Rack-chair. Type of folding chair.

Rail. Horizontal section of framework holding a panel.

Ratchet. Set of angular or saw-like teeth on the edge of a bar or wheel into which a cog, click or pawl may engage.

Raven's Head. Classical motif used by Robert Adam.

Rebate. Rectangular channel on the edge of framing or of a drawer.

Recessed Carving. Method of producing a raised pattern, much used by joiners in the 17th century.

Reed-and-tie Moulding. Ornamentation simulating ribbons.

Reeded, Reeding. As fluting but with ornament in relief. Derived from classical column.

Refectory Table

Example of Reeding

Restoration Chair   **Rising Sun Ornament**   **Ribband-back Chair**

Refectory Table. A colloquialism for long-table. The refectory was the room in religious houses or colleges where meals were served.

Regence Style. Transitional French period style between baroque and rococo.

Regency. Description strictly applied to furniture, architecture, etc., from the period of the Regency (1810–20). In fact the term is frequently used in describing the period 1800–30.

Reggivaso. 18th-century vase stand made in a variety of forms —e.g. satyrs, chained negro slaves, etc.

Renaissance. Classical revival which originated in Italy in the 14th/15th century and spread through Europe, reaching England in the early 16th century.

Repoussé. Ornamental metalwork hammered into relief form from the reverse side.

Restoration Furniture. So-called after the Restoration of Charles II. Chairs were elaborately carved and scrolled, their backs often surmounted by crowns, or boys and crowns.

Ribband-back Chair. Mahogany chair with carved splat in form of knotted ribbons and bows.

Rising Sun Ornament. Found on late 18th-century American

251

Romayne   **Rudd's Table**   **Saddle Seat**

case furniture. Carved ornament intended to represent the rays of the rising sun.

Robing Mirror. A large long mirror.

Rocaille. French word (originally meaning rock-work) from which derives the term rococo (q.v.).

Rocking Chair. Simply constructed chair, mounted on rockers, probably of American invention. Authentic 'slat-back' examples reliably date back to 1800, though claims have been made to as early an initial date as 1650–1700. In America, where the chair has long been a familiar institution, there exists such local types as the Boston, Salem and Windsor rocking chairs.

Rococo. Style of decoration originating in France and Italy in the late 17th century and prevalent in Europe until c. 1770. Characterised especially by scroll work, shell motifs, asymmetrical effects and light colouring.

Roll-top Desk. Resembles cylinder-top desk except that the 'roll down' section is slatted.

Romayne. Medallion heads in profile found on early Tudor furniture.

Roundabout Chair. See CORNER CHAIR.

Rounded Ends. Early Chippendale chairs were sometimes made with their top rail rounded at the ends, in the Queen Anne style.

Roundel. Small decorative disc or medallion.

Rudd's Table. A kind of dressing table, first introduced by Thomas Shearer and subsequently improved upon by Sheraton and Hepplewhite. Constructed with a complexity of hinged mirrors to enable ladies to see their faces and the back of their heads simultaneously.

Runner. American term, alternative to rocking chair.

Rush Seat. Seat woven of rushes. Much used with country furniture. Popular in America from earliest times.

Sabre Leg. Sharp outward curved leg of chair or settee, in classical style. Late 18th and early 19th century.

Salem Secretary

Saddle Seat. Late 18th-century seat, gently curving and sloping down in the centre.

Salem Rocker. Early 19th-century rocking chair, made at Salem, Mass.

Salem Secretary. American bureau with china cabinet above, made at Salem, Mass.

Salem Snowflake. Six-pointed punched decoration resembling snowflake on Salem furniture.

Sample Chair. A miniature chair, used by craftsmen as a sample of the full-sized one.

Sand-box. Vase-shaped box for sprinkling sand on wet ink. See also POUNCEBOX.

Sanded. Wood that has been sanded to give a rough effect.

'Savonarola' Chair. As X chairs (q.v.) but with struts following the curve of the design.

Sawbuck Table. American table with X-shaped frame.

Scole Chair. Variety of WINDSOR CHAIR.

Sconce. Wall light with back-plate and tray or branched candle-holders.

Scoop Pattern. Gouged band in wood with rounded top and, sometimes, rounded base.

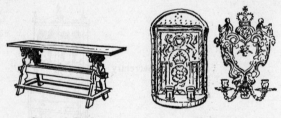

Sawbuck Table   Sconces

Scratch Carved. Also known as incised carving; single outline scratched on surface of wood.

Screen Stick. Tripod base to pole screen.

Screen Table. Table with writing slide and adjustable screen to protect the writer from the heat of the fire.

Scroll Foot. Terminal to leg of chair in form of carved scroll fashionable in the 18th century.

Scrutoire or Escritoire. Writing cabinet with let-down front forming writing surface, drawers and pigeon holes above and chest of drawers or stand below.

Scutcheon. Shield engraved with armorial bearings.

Examples of Scroll Foot.   Scrutoire.   Seaweed Marquetry

Seaweed Marquetry. Marquetry in the form of sprays of seaweed, found on clock cases, cabinets and table tops. Early 18th century.

Secretaire. Piece of furniture for keeping private papers, etc., with writing shelf.

Secretaire Bookcase. Piece of furniture with shelves above, a desk closed by a drop front, and a cupboard below.

Serpentine-fronted. Applied to cabinet furniture second half of 18th century; undulating front (convex flanked by two concave curves).

Secretaire

Serpentine-fronted

Settee   **Settle**

Serre-papier. Writing table accessory to hold paper. Also called CARTONNIER.

Settee. Long seat with back and usually arms, for more than one person.

Settle. Bench with high back and arms and frequently with box or chest under seat.

Sewing Table. Small table with drawers; frequently also with cloth bag to contain sewing. Late 18th century.

Shaker Furniture. Term applied to all kinds of furniture made by a 19th-century American religious sect called the Shakers.

Shell Ornament. 18th-century motif applied to furniture; also to porcelain, silverware, etc.

Shepherd's Crook Arm. 18th-century design of chair or settee arm.

Shell Ornaments

Shepherd's Crook Arm

Shield-shaped Back   **Sideboard**   **Slat-back Chair**

Shield-shaped Back. Chair with uprights in form of a shield, with carved and pierced splat. Late 18th century.

Side-rails. Vertical members at back of chair. Also called UPRIGHTS.

Sideboard. As the name suggests, a side-board or table for the display of plate, foodstuffs, etc., which evolved into a more elaborate piece of furniture, with drawers and storage cupboards scarcely distinguishable from a dresser.

Skeleton Frame. A very fine, narrow frame, often used on looking glasses.

Slant-front Desk. Frame or chest of drawers, the top section acting as a desk with a hinged lid sloped at an angle of 45 degrees when closed. Known in England as a bureau.

Slat-back Chair. 17th-century chair with horizontal slats at back. Precursor of the 18th-century ladder-back.

Sleigh Bed. 19th-century American bed, with especially high boards top and bottom, usually terminating in scroll-shaped rails.

Slider. A receptacle of silver, papier-mâché or mahogany for moving wine, beer or food about the dining table. Also known as COASTER.

Typical Sofa

Sofa Table

Sofa. Long seat with raised back and end(s).

Sofa Table. Rectangular table with hinged leaves at each end; sometimes with two front drawers. Late 18th century.

Spade Foot. Late 18th-century rectangular tapering foot.

Spandrel. Space between curve and arch of frame in which it is contained.

Spanish Foot. Late 17th-century terminal for chair or settee, scroll-form with curving ribs.

Spinet. See VIRGINAL.

Spinning Wheel. Simple apparatus, worked either by hand or foot, for the manufacture of yarn or thread. Dating from the earliest times, and still much in use in rural areas throughout the 19th century.

Splat. Flat piece of wood forming central part of chairback.

Splayed Leg. Outward sloping leg.

Splint Seat. Seat made of oak and hickory strips interlaced. 18th-century country furniture.

Split Baluster. Found on oak furniture of the mid-17th century, sometimes accompanied by applied jewel or lozenge ornament.

Spool Turning. Ornament applied to 19th-century American Empire table legs, and head and foot boards of beds. Effect resembles row of spools.

Spoon Rack. Miniature dresser with slotted shelves for hanging spoons and accommodation below for knives and forks.

Spade Foot   **Spanish Foot**   **Spinning Wheel**   **Spool Turning**

Originally dating from Tudor times, was still in use at the end of the 18th century.

Spoon-back Chair. American term for Queen Anne chair with back curved like a spoon.

Spring Top. A spring catch, found on Davenports, to release the stationery section.

Stencilling. Introduced in the first half of the 19th century. Applied to furniture in the customary manner, with a brush and stencil-cut, heavy water-proof paper.

Spoon Rack   **Standish**

Strapwork Ornament   **Stretcher**   **Example of Stringing**

Stick Chair. See WINDSOR CHAIR.

Stickwork. Made by fixing adhesive fillets of different-coloured woods together to form a patterned block.

Stile. The outside vertical section of a frame.

Stool. Small, backless seat.

Strapwork Ornament. Ornament of interlaced ribbon and scrollwork, with the occasional addition of foliage. Late 16th, early 17th century.

Straw-work. Decoration of small items of furniture with strips of bleached and coloured straw to form patterns.

Stretcher. Horizontal member connecting chair or table legs.

Stringing. Inlay arranged in narrow lines.

Stripping. The removal of the original surface of a piece of furniture down to the wood.

Strozzi Stool. Three-legged stool with octagonal seat and high, narrow back. Made in Tuscany in the 15th century.

Stumpwork. Raised embroidery, parts of which are padded; sometimes found on mirror frames.

Sunburst. English derivation of the rising sun motif much employed in the ornamentation of American furniture.

Sunflower. Popular subject for ornamental carving on Connecticut desks and chairs, and other pieces of American furniture of earliest manufacture.

Sunk Carving. See RECESSED CARVING.

Sutherland Table. Narrow-topped table with deep falling flaps.

Strozzi Stool   **Stumpwork**   **Example of Swags**

Swags. Late 17th- and early 18th-century decorative motif; festoons of flowers, fruits and leaves.

Swan-necked Pediment. Curved scroll motif found on Georgian bureau and bookcases. See also BROKEN PEDIMENT.

Swing-leg Table. American term to differentiate from gate-leg table.

Table of Degree. Precursor of the COURT CUPBOARD. Tiered stand for the display of plate.

Table Chair (or Bench). Incorrectly described as Monk's chair. Convertible chair with pivot-back which can be made into a table.

Table Chair

Tabouret. French term for a stool.

Tallboy. Tall chest of drawers, occasionally in two sections—one above the other.

Tarsia. Italian marquetry, very popular in the 15th century, made up of wood, bone, metal and mother-of-pearl.

Tavern Table. For service in 18th-century taverns. Small, strongly made table, the legs of which were usually braced with stretchers. Often made with the addition of a drawer or two in the apron.

Tallboy

Tavern Table

Tea-poy

Tea or Games Table. A table with a folding top enclosing a well, which could contain a backgammon board. When closed it could be used as a tea table.

Tea-poy. A tea chest on a stand, with an opening at the top, rather like a work table. It should not be confused with a tea canister.

Tear-drop Handle. Late 16th- early 17th-century handle hanging from brass plate and attached by wire pins. See DROP HANDLE.

Tenon. Principal joint used by joiners from the 16th century. Fills in the mortice cavity.

Tester. Wooden canopy over four-poster bed.

Till. Fitted tray in 17th-century chest.

Toaster. Three-pronged fork for toasting bread or meat. Rarer examples are standing toasters with central pillar and tripod base.

Toilet Mirror. Small mirror made to stand on table. Mostly late 17th century.

Torchère. Late 17th-century candle or lamp stand.

Trail Ornament. Found on oak furniture of the 17th century; running border pattern of leaf spray or tendril.

Treen. Descriptive of a variety of small wooden articles.

Trespolo. Three-legged table designed to carry small *objets d'art* or a candlestick; usually standing against a wall. 18th century.

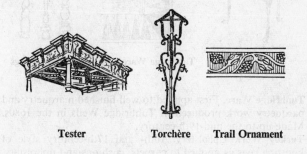

| Tester | Torchère | Trail Ornament |

Trevails. Old term descriptive of cylindrical wooden fastening pins.

Tricoteuse. Small work-table with gallery, part of which may be lowered to house knitting and sewing materials. Probably of 19th-century origin.

Tripod Legs. See PEDESTAL TABLE.

Trivet. Stand for kettle, placed over a fire, originally on three feet. Later examples have projection which secure the trivet on the top bar of the grate.

Trussing Coffers. Leather-covered travelling chests.

Tuckaway Table. American gate-leg table, the legs of which fold into each other.

Tudor Style. From 1485 to 1603; marked the transition from the Gothic tradition.

Tumblers. Bolt-retaining units in a lock mechanism.

| Trivet | Tunbridge Ware Design | Turned Legs |

Tunbridge Ware. First applied to well-finished marquetry and parquetry work produced in Tunbridge Wells in the 1680s. Made up to the mid-19th century.

Turkey Work Upholstery. 16th- and 17th-century style of knotting rugs as applied to carpets, cushions and upholstery.

Turned Legs. Several varieties are found on chairs and tables, including twist-turned, bobbin-turned, baluster-turned, etc. Made with the use of a pole lathe.

Turtle-back. Decorative boss in shape of turtle's back found on Jacobean-style cupboards.

Twist Turning. Derivation from the Flemish single rope and the English double rope style. 17th century.

Urn Stand

Vargueno

Universal Table. Late 18th-century dining table with extending draw leaves.

Uprights. The outside verticals of a chair back.

Urn Stand. In form of small table on three or four legs; also metal-lined box with side opening for kettle spout. Late 17th century. See also KETTLE STAND.

Vargueno. Spanish, fall-front cabinet, with drawers. Frequently mounted on stand.

Vauxhall Plate. Mirror-plate made from mid-17th to late 18th century at Vauxhall glasshouse.

Veneer. Thin sheets of delicately figured wood glued to the surface of the furniture to be so decorated.

Virginal. Resembling a spinet, with single string to each note, operating with a plucking device like the harpsichord.

Virginal

Vitruvian Scroll. Band of repeated scrolls forming an ornamental border; used in architecture and furniture decoration in the 18th century, and later on carpets and metalwork.

Voider. Medieval term for a tray.

Volutes. Twin spiral scrolls, used in architecture on the Ionic capital and applied in the decoration of furniture.

Wagon Seat. American. Double seat with twin backs, slatted or Windsor type, used for sitting out of doors.

Wainscot. Familiarly associated with wall panelling, usually of oak, but at a very early date applied to pieces of furniture such as bedsteads, chairs, stools, etc., which were described as being of 'wainscot'.

Wainscot Chair. Panel-backed chair of late 16th and early 17th century.

Vitruvian Scroll   **Voider**

Wall-bracket. Used for display of china, busts, etc., and for accommodating clocks, candlesticks, etc. From end of 17th century.

Wall-lights. See SCONCE.

Ward. Element in a lock which prevents it being turned by any but the correct key.

Wardrobe. Evolved in late 17th century from early cupboard and cabinet. Upright and enclosed by doors, customarily ornamented on exterior, with shelves and hanging space.

Warming Pan. For warming beds; metal, usually copper, pan with long handle.

Wagon Seat   **Wainscot Chair**   **Wall-bracket**

Washing-stand. Introduced into the bedroom after 1750; either on a tripod with circular top and fitted basin, or on four legs with cupboards or drawers below and a lid covering the sunk basin.

Water Leaf. Ornamental carved leaf motif.

Web Foot. American term for three-toed or Dutch foot. Also Drake or Duck foot.

Wardrobe   **Warming Pan**   **Washing-stands**

What-not

Windsor Chairs

Wellington Chest. Tall, narrow chest with about twelve drawers, all of which can be locked together by the provision of an overall hinged flap.

Welsh Dresser. Intended for the display of plate, having shelves above and drawers below, enclosed by one or two doors.

What-not. Open stand with several shelves for displaying knick-knacks, etc.

Wheat-ear Ornament. Motif often used on late 18th-century chairbacks.

Whorl. Circular decorative ornament used on medieval furniture. See also ROUNDEL.

Windsor Chair. Having wooden saddle seat, with turned spindles at back and turned and splayed legs. From the 18th century. See also STICK CHAIR.

Wine Cooler. Case, often mahogany, for containing ice or water for cooling wine.

Wing Bookcase. Bookcase in which the central section protrudes beyond the side, or 'wing' sections. Mid-18th century.

Wing Chair. Found in England from the 17th century. High-backed, upholstered chairs, with arms and wing protrusions on either side of the back.

Wine Cooler

Wing Chair

Work Table

Winthrop Desk. Chippendale style slant-top desk, named after a 17th-century Governor of Massachusetts.

Work Table. Name given to tables made for ladies' needlework in second half of the 18th century.

Worm-hole. Effected by a variety of wood-boring beetles inexplicably known as 'worms'.

Writing Cabinet. Has fall-front and a number of small drawers. From the latter part of the 16th century.

Writing Table. Knee-hole version introduced in the early 18th century. Those of greater elegance made at the end of the 18th century. Many examples were frequently used as side or card tables. From the late 17th century.

Writing Table

X-Chair   X-Stool   Yorkshire Chair

Writing-box Stand. The post-Restoration writing box, sometimes with drawers below, was provided with a gate-legged stand on which the box was placed rather than on the table.

X-chair. Having an X-shaped frame, the seat and back covered with fabric. From medieval times.

X-stool. Folding stool made on the same principle as X-chairs.

Yorkshire Chair. Oak chair with back of ornamented hoop rails or with arcaded open back. Mid-17th century.

PART SIX

Carpets

Abadeh. Persian carpets with floral patterns and, usually, blue or ivory background, resembling fine Afshari (q.v.) carpets.

Abi-I-Sangar. Persian name for 'stone-blue' although, in fact, the colour that is characteristic in the borders of these carpets is a greyish-green which, because of the dye used, tends to wear down, giving the other border colours the appearance of relief.

Acanthus. Classical motif of conventional foliage probably borrowed by the Persians for their carpet designs.

Afghan. Name applied to most coarse or medium-quality carpets made in Afghanistan. Design consists invariably of identical polygons; colours are predominantly brownish-red with the addition of indigo and, occasionally, cucumber-green to the natural white of the wool.

Afghan-Charpay. Small bedside rugs in the Afghan polygonal pattern.

Afghan-Hatchlou. Used both as prayer-rugs and as tent curtains.

Afshari. Made by nomad tribes 40 miles from Kirman in south-east Iran. Brightly coloured rugs both in a coarse texture and in silky wool.

Agra. Open fields of olive green, blue, fawn, and tan with medallions and corners. Usually in extra large sizes. The Taj Mahal is in Agra.

Ahskali. Pattern of lozenges and cross-bars employed by the Kashkais on the borders of their carpets.

Akhissar. Coarse, brightly coloured rugs from this district of Anatolia, usually with geometrical patterns.

Alentours. Descriptive of borders of tapestries.

Allover. Term for repetitive design on carpet having no medallions.

Anatolian Rugs. Term generally applied to all Turkish rugs. Anatolian prayer-rugs occupy a special category.

Animal Carpets. Of the classical period, portraying hunting scenes or animals. Probably made in Tabriz or Ispahan.

Arab-Beloutch. Coarse-textured carpets made by the Beloutchi nomads.

Arabesque. Medallion-like ornament with four opposite branching tendrils.

Animal motif

Arabesque ornament

Ardebil Rugs. From Iran. In colours and geometrical design similar to the old Caucasian rugs. Not to be confused with the Ardebil Mosque Carpet, one of the most celebrated in the world, which may be seen at the Victoria and Albert Museum.

Armenian Red. Cochineal dye prepared from species of shell insect found in Karapapagh.

Armenian Shirvan. Rugs produced by the Russians over the last thirty or forty years in the Armenian districts of the Caucasus.

Arras Tapestry. The celebrated Arras tapestries were produced in the 14th and 15th centuries.

Asia Minor Rugs. All Turkish rugs were once referred to as Asia Minor rugs.

Assisi-work. In which the ground is covered in long-armed cross-stitch, leaving the pattern displayed in plain linen.

Astana. Village near Sultanabad, in Iraq, where carpets called Sarouks are produced.

Aubusson Carpets. Made at Aubusson in France in the 18th and 19th centuries. The majority have a cream field and include delicate tones of rose, tan, plum, green, wisteria and blue in the design. Also clusters of roses.

Aubusson Tapestry. Made at Aubusson in France in the 18th and 19th centuries.

Axminster Carpets. Carpets of cut pile made by a variety of processes, originally at Axminster, in Devon, in imitation of hand-knotted oriental carpets.

Bagshaish. Descriptive of two types of Persian carpet of glossy wool made near Lake Urmia.

Bahktiari Rugs. Made in a large number of villages in Iran, usually with panels containing flowers, or with floral medallions.

Baku Rugs. Caucasian. Characteristic design: blue field with large angular pears in rows.

Balkan Rugs. Made in Bulgaria, almost indistinguishable from Persian Tabriz rugs.

Balughistan Rugs. Made in Iran and Afghanistan by the Baluchi tribes on horizontal looms; characterised by the use of rather sombre reds and purplish-blue effects.

Bam. Bam rugs are made in the city of Bampur in Iran. Floral in design, they are distinguished for the rare use of moss-green as a colour.

Bayasid. City on the Iran-Turkish border long noted for the production of carpets of Persian design.

Beauvais Carpets. Knotted pile carpets in the Savonnerie manner were made at Beauvais between 1780–92 and, again, in the Napoleonic period.

Beauvais Tapestry. Made for hangings and upholstery at Beauvais in the 17th and 18th centuries. These celebrated tapestries commanded the best designers of the Courts of Louis XIV, XV, and XVI.

Bergamo Rugs. Made in Turkey. Richly coloured, lustrous and deep-piled, diversely patterned but usually with central medallion fringed with latch hooks.

Beshir Rugs. The large sizes have a wine-coloured field and, frequently, an allover angular floral design in blue, green and yellow.

Bid-Medschnun. Descriptive of most Central Persian carpets with design of poplars and weeping willows.

Bijar. Tightly woven, thick pile Persian carpet, made in many different designs.

Bird Carpets. Name used in the trade for Ouchak carpets made in the 17th century.

Biredchend. Kind of Khorassan carpet, usually patterned with medallions and of a light purplish red colour.

Bokhara. Frequently used to cover all Turkoman rugs; woven in the Tekke design, usually with wine-red field.

Bokhara-Hatchlou. Turkoman rugs designed with four fields divided by a cross.

Bokhara-Palas. Hard, rough-textured carpets with repetitive geometrical patterns. Made with a red field and with dark blue as the principal extra colour.

Border. Accessory guards. The narrower borders that accompany the main border round the majority of Persian carpets.

Bordshali-Kasak. Thick-piled Caucasian rugs, with glossy wool and coloured with the best quality vegetable dyes.

Borlou. Medium-quality Turkish carpet mostly coloured with artificial dyes.

Boutique D'or. 17th-century Paris tapestry factory of De La Planche and Comans.

Brussa. Best known for the production of brightly and artistically coloured prayer-rugs, also finely knotted carpets.

Brussels Carpets. See MOQUETTE.

Brussels Tapestry. Brussels was the leading centre of tapestry making throughout the 16th, 17th and 18th centuries. Designs include the extravagant baroque of the 17th century, subjects from Roman and Biblical history, woodland scenes, etc.

Buckthorn. Buckthorn berries are widely used in the East in the preparation of an orange-yellow dye.

Carriage Carpets. Small rugs stuffed, usually with cotton waste, to serve as cushions in the two-wheeled carts used in China and other parts of the East.

Caucasian Carpets. Carpets have been produced in the Caucasus probably since the Turkish infiltration of the 9th and 11th centuries.

Central Motif. Design motif based on the circle with extended elements reaching out symmetrically in all directions.

Cesarea (Kaiserea). Anatolian centre from which many modern carpets are produced, known in Europe under a variety of names.

Chadours (Chaudors). Rugs of the Bokhara family, chestnut brown in colour.

Charpays. Translated, means 'four-foot'. The term is used in descriptions of the smaller Afghan rugs.

Chi. Ornament which has been ascribed to the Chinese symbol of immortality, the 'sacred sponge'; resembles the 'bank of clouds'.

Chila. Fine Shirvan carpets, mostly in floral designs, often with stylised birds in the corners or borders.

Chinese Carpets. May chiefly be identified by their naturalistic flower patterns, Chinese 'good luck' signs, 'key pattern' and swastika ornaments.

Chintamani. Buddhist symbol consisting of three balls in shape of a triangle.

Chosrau. See 'SPRINGTIDE IN CHOSRAU'.

Chotan. Chotan carpets are frequently described as Samarkand carpets, from the time when they were bought and sold in the great bazaar at Samarkand. Finer than those made in Kashgar, they are usually madder-red and dark blue in colour and sometimes employ Chinese motifs.

Chourdjin. A saddle-bag. Chourdjins are usually made in fine designs, beautifully coloured.

Cloudband ornament

Chouval. Bag used by the Turkomans for storing various articles, normally hung inside their tents.

Cloudband. Ornament in the shape of a wriggling worm, frequently found on the knotted carpets of the 16th century.

Cotton Carpets from Yesd. Simple, mostly geometrically patterned knotted carpets of cotton yarn made in and around Yesd.

Crenellated Motif. Geometrical motif which in its more recent form consists of alternating lozenge-shaped figures emerging from triangles.

Daghestan Rugs. Produced in the north-eastern Caucasus. Closely resemble Shirvan rugs; mostly red and blue or cream.

Damascus Rugs. So-called because they were shipped through the port of Damascus; in fact, it has been established that they were made in Turkey. Mostly geometrical in design, using cherry red, light blue, yellow and sage green, they are woven from Angora wool.

Demirdschi. City in Asia Minor where prayer-rugs were made in the 17th and 18th centuries, and later.

Derband Rugs. See DAGHESTAN RUGS.

Djabrail (or Chabrail). Made in the Caucasus; distinguished for their design of pear-shaped palm-tree tops, varying from four to eight inches high.

Djefti. The Lour dwarf oak from which almost all the brown dyes are obtained.

Djidjim. Of cotton embroidered in wool, made in Smyrna and usually used as a material covering for sofas, etc. Because of its extreme cheapness was sold in enormous quantities in Europe early in this century.

Djoshegan. Persian carpets, having palmette motifs, with blue and deep red predominating, and unusual method of knotting, the yarn embracing four rather than two warp threads.

Djuft. Persian name for pair. Bedside rugs and runners are usually made in pairs.

Do-Gule. Persian name for 'two blossoms'. The pattern appears mostly in Gerus carpets.

Donegal Carpets. Coarse knotted carpets first made in Donegal, Ireland, at the end of the 19th century. Pile carpets are still made at Donegal.

Dosar. Persian measurement. 'Two sars' is approximately 7ft.

Dowletabad. Small town near Hamadan, producing closely woven carpets not dissimilar from Saruks.

Dragon Carpets. Dragons are frequently depicted on carpets in a variety of forms. It is believed that the celebrated Caucasian Dragon carpets incorporate the motif of an animal pelt, not a dragon, as was always assumed.

Druja. Persian term meaning 'two faces' and having a particular application to Kilim carpets, the backs of which are indistinguishable from the fronts.

Dughi (or Turkey Red). Obtained from madder roots with the addition of sour milk curds.

Enessy. The curtains which Turkomans hang before the entrance of their tents.

Erivan. City in the South Caucasus, where are made Kasak and Gendje-type carpets and finely woven Palases.

Ersaris. Turkoman tribe who knot carpets in geometrical patterns, with large polygons, which are predominantly a dark purplish red in colour.

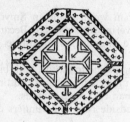

Ersaris pattern

Forked Tendrils

Eski-Kirman. Carpets dating back to the late 18th and early 19th century in Turkey; mostly having a cream-coloured ground and medallions.

Eski-Shehir. Good, medium-quality Turkish carpet, light in colour with designs usually based on traditional Persian patterns. Often called 'Sparta' or 'Isparta' carpets.

Everted Calyx. Motif frequently used in the design of Persian carpets; two sepals of a calyx bent right and left, the points turned downwards and a bud between them.

Exeter Carpets. Expensive hand-knotted carpets made by Claude Passavant, a native of Basel, who set up in Exeter as a merchant and manufacturer in the mid-18th century.

Exote. Term loosely applied in Austria to long, narrow Persian carpets. Meaning 'exotic' it was also frequently used to describe carpets of unknown origin.

Farsibaff. Meaning: 'Persian knots'. Applied to Khorassan carpets made in and around Meshed.

Felt Carpets. Made in Persia; sold locally. Composed of undyed sheep's wool and possibly also camel-hair. Without pattern or decoration.

Feraghan Rugs. First examples date from the second half of the 18th century. Some have small over-all design, others a central medallion. The more valuable have an apple-green main border, as opposed to a rose or blue border.

Fes-Hané. Carpets of the Hereke type were made here in the days of Sultan Abdul Hamid.

Field, The. The area of a carpet which lies within the four borders.

Field, Divided. The field of oriental carpets is often divided by cross-bars, shields, etc.

Findighan. Fine carpets produced in the Shirvan district and in the southern Caucasus, decorated with scattered flowers the size of hazel-nuts.

Florentine Armorial Tapestry. Bearing the arms of the House of Medici.

Forked Tendrils. Tendrils with outspread ends; a characteristic of Herati borders.

Foyer. Turkish hall-rug.

Fringes. The severed warp-threads at either end of a carpet which are knotted to prevent fraying.

Gall-apples. Or oak-apples, used in the production of dark brown tones.

Galleries. 19th-century Viennese term for runners.

Garden Carpets. Term for Persian antique carpets with designs of flower-beds, garden paths, stylised birds, etc.

Gendje Rugs. Frequently mistaken for Kazaks; Caucasian rugs with diagonal stripes over the whole field.

Gentleman's Carpet. Term applied to quietly coloured and patterned carpets of subtle beauty—often to the older Feraghan, Sarabend and Mir carpets.

Gerus Carpets. Produced near the city of Bidjar; lustrous wool, deep-piled, coloured with bright vegetable dyes.

Ghali. Name applied to every carpet in Persia.

Ghalidshé. Diminutive of Ghalid; name in Persia for small carpet.

Ghiordes Knot. Species of knot used in many oriental carpets.

Ghiordes Rugs. Prayer rugs produced in the city of that name in Asia Minor since the 17th century. Closely knotted and closely clipped, with borders of small flowers or narrow stripes of colour.

Gilans. Name given to Caucasian knotted carpets from the neighbourhood of Kuba.

Gobelins, Manufacture Royale des. Founded in Louis XIV's reign and supported by the State, for the production of fine tapestries; also furniture and other works of art.

Greek Carpets. Knotted carpets were made by the Greeks from the earliest times, but were not marketed abroad until after the Greco-Turkish war.

Gul-henna. 'Henna-blossom.' Plant yielding a red dye, often seen as main motif of 'allover' patterns (q.v.).

Gul-I-Shiraz. 'Rose of Shiraz.' Stylised flower pattern.

Hamadan. The Persian city and the district surrounding it is one of the largest rug-weaving centres in the country. Made in a great variety of designs, they are often thick and heavy rugs, noted for their durability.

Hatschlou. Representation of a cross. Carpets of this name are made in Central Asia, the cross dividing them into four compartments.

Herat Rugs. Herat was once the capital of Afghanistan, when it was the centre of a great carpet industry. The Herati design consists of two rosettes of lanceolate leaves, the border being

Ghiordes knot

Herati design

composed of palmettes turning inwards and outwards alternately. Predominant colours were deep dark blue and madder-red.

Hereke Carpets. Carpets were originally woven at Hereke in a factory owned by the Sultan Abdul Hamid. Persian designs were copied; also French designs of the reigns of Louis XV and XVI. In many the pile was shorn in small areas so as to give an effect of relief.

Herez. Important carpet and rug-producing centre 40 miles east of Tabriz. Imported into Europe and America in large numbers. Herez and Georavan rugs and carpets usually have in common designs composed of a large, geometrically-shaped medallion against a red, rose, or rust field covered with angular floral patterns in blue, pink, green, ivory, brown, tinges of canary, and plum.

Hila Rugs. Caucasian rugs, usually ice-blue in colour with small centre medallion and matching corner-pieces.

Hispano-Mauresque. Closely akin to the Seljuk carpets, these were made in Spain in Moorish times.

Holbein Carpets. Old Turkish carpets imported into Europe throughout the 15th century; so-called because they may be seen in some of Holbein's paintings. Designs were purely geometric.

Holy Carpet. See ARDEBIL RUGS.

Hunting Carpets. Persian carpets of great beauty with hunting scene designs were made in the 16th century. Inferior carpets with a similar motif still appear from time to time.

Ibrahimabad. Village near Sultanabad where Mahal carpets of medium quality are made.

Indian Carpets. Indian carpets made in all sizes, mainly for export, are all based on Persian traditions.

Indigo. Low-growing plant or shrub, treated to yield a fast blue dye.

Intermittent Wavy Shoots and Wavy Tendrils, etc. Characteristic design of the narrow parallel guards of a carpet.

Iris. See HEREZ (or Heris) of which it is a corruption.

Ispahan Rugs. The rarest Ispahan carpets were made in the 16th and 17th centuries and exist only in museums and private collections. The so-called Ispahans made in this century come from in and around the city of Meshed, and are technically named Turkibaffs. Their main colour is cochineal red; some have allover designs, others a variety of medallions.

Isparta. See ESKI-SHEHIR.

Italy. Pope Clement XI founded a carpet-weaving factory at San Michele, Rome, in the early 18th century. The carpets were made in the Savonnerie manner, derived from the Turkish. Peasants in the Abruzzi highlands and in Sardinia still weave rugs, but these are really intended as bed covers.

Jelabird (Chelabird, Tshelabird). Name given to Caucasian rugs bearing a device resembling an eagle with outstretched wings.

Joshaghan Rugs. Persian rugs, the general design of which has not altered for two hundred years. This design is composed of small angular floral patterns in the shape of diamonds, either repeated over the whole field or featured as a centrepiece.

Jugoslavia. Kelim (q.v.) or tapestry woven rugs were produced in Bosnia, Serbia and the Banat throughout the 19th century.

Kabistan. Trade name for fine Shirvan (q.v.) rugs.

Kalemkar. Persian term for 'crayon work'. Formerly applied to native—later to imported—cotton fabrics printed by hand. Found on shawls and light prayer-rugs carried by travellers in a saddle-bag.

Intermittent Wavy Shoots

Kar-Hané. Workshop or factory in which carpets are woven.

Karabagh Rugs. Have been described as the floral-patterned version of the Kazaks. Karabaghs and Kazaks are considered the best of the thick Caucasian rugs.

Karadagh. Frequently pass by the name of 'Ardebils' (q.v.).

Karaghöz. Name given to carpets made by the Karaghuzlu nomads. Predominantly coloured dark brown and darkest indigo, they employ a modified form of the Feraghan design.

Karaja Rugs. Generally coloured like Herez rugs (q.v.), with three geometric medallions and small floral designs over the rest of the field.

Karamani. Term used in the Istanbul market to describe Kelims, flat woven carpets made in Persia and Central Asia.

Karkus. The carpets of the Kirghiz (q.v.).

Kars. Caucasian carpets akin to the Kazaks, with a specially thick pile and usually oblong in shape, were once made at Kars, on the Persian-Kurdish frontier.

Kashan Rugs. The original Kashan rugs were made with merino wool and were rated at one time the finest and costliest of all new oriental rugs. The distinguishing characteristic of the Kashan is its very close knotting. The most favoured design in the later period is an arabesque medallion, with appropriate corners.

Kashgar Rugs. Coarsely textured, short-piled rugs, in design much influenced by the Chinese; used by the Turks to lay on benches as well as for floor coverings, or to spread over layers of hay or straw in their two-wheeled carts.

Kashkai. The Kashkais are one of the largest Persian tribes, and together with a number of neighbouring tribes make Shiraz carpets, or as they are sometimes called 'Meccas'. They are all wool and have a silky lustre.

Kashmir. Hand-knotted and embroidered carpets have been made in Kashmir since the end of the last century. Soumak (q.v.) rugs are known also as Kashmir.

Kasvin. Persian carpets, very finely knotted, patterned with an endlessly repeated geometric design.

Kazak Rugs. Thick-piled Caucasian rugs with geometric designs and a field often divided into three connecting panels.

Keleï. Derived from *Ghali*, the Persian for 'carpet'.

Kelims. Made in Persia, Caucasia, Turkey and Asia Minor; they are double-faced, smooth with a flat stitch on both sides.

Kenabend. Dimensional reference to narrow bedside rugs made in and around Tabriz.

Kenaré. Persian word for 'shore, edge'. Kenaré runners are so called because of the peculiar arrangement of carpets in Iran; one carpet forms the centrepiece, another is placed at its head, and a Kenaré at either side.

Kerki. Fine quality Afghan carpets are made at Kerki; they bear a large, divided octagon and their background is usually cherry- or ox-blood red.

Kermes. Persian name for cochineal.

Kewsur. See SEICHUR.

Khain (Ghain). City of Khorassan. Most of the Khain carpets are Keleïs. The various design elements consist of Herati designs, medallions, and sometimes animals.

Khilin. An idealised animal form often represented in Chinese art.

Khiva Rugs. Virtually identical in appearance with Afghans; design comprises rows of octagons and the predominant colour is usually wine-red.

Khorassan Carpets. Old Khorassans, now very rare, were compactly woven and especially silky. Those made since the 1920s are coarser and, though beautiful in their designs, relatively inexpensive.

Kiaba. Caucasian term denoting a particular size of carpet, namely 4 feet to 4 feet 8 inches by 9 feet 4 inches to 10 feet 6 inches. Often used as a prefix to a specific carpet to denote size, e.g. Kiaba-Shirvan.

Kibitka Strips. Or Bokhara-bands. Woven or hand-knotted material used by some of the Turkoman tribes to decorate the inside of their Kibitkas, or tent-like huts.

Kidderminster Rugs. Made at one of the oldest centres of rug-making in Britain, these were originally almost pileless. In 1753 Brussels carpets (or moquette to use the Continental term) were introduced to compete with Wilton.

Kilimdjé. Diminutive of Kilim or Kelim (q.v.).

Kilimlik. End border woven in the style of Kelims (q.v.).

Kilmarnock Carpets. Double-cloth carpeting was made in Kilmarnock from the third quarter of the 18th century; three-ply was perfected in 1824.

Kirghiz Carpets. Coarse to medium textured carpets made by the Kirghiz, who live between the Russo-Chinese frontier and Tashkent. Rarely available in Europe.

Kirman Rugs. Kirmans are made in many qualities; the field is usually cream or ivory and the design is in pastel colours—similar to many Indian rugs. Kirman is one of the major Iranian cities.

Kirman-Lavers. Similar to Kirmans (q.v.) but more coarsely woven.

Kirmanshah. The Kirmanshah bazaar is on the great caravan route to Baghdad. Certain carpets, especially the Keleïs, are often given this name. They are predominantly moss-green and copper in colour.

Kirshehir. See ESKI-SHEHIR.

Kis-Ghiordes. A kind of sofa rug, customarily with a dull cream ground and a pattern mainly of blue and heliotrope.

Kis-Kelim. Diminutive, meaning little Kelims (q.v.).

Kisil-Ajak; 'Golden foot'. Name given to very fine-quality dark and reddish-brown carpets produced by the Turkomans in Central Asia.

Knotted Pile Carpets. English examples date from the 16th and 17th centuries, but floor carpets were not in general use until the 18th century. Previously they were imported from the Near East, but used principally to cover tables, chests, etc., and to place before the altar in a church or chapel.

Koltuk. Name applied by the Persians to rugs from Kurdistan with a deep pile and colouring reminiscent of the old Feraghan carpets.

Konia. An Anatolian carpet produced from the early 17th to mid-18th century; usually with geometric design comprising broad zig-zag bands.

Kuba Rugs. Kabistan rugs produced in this century are really Kubas; the Russians call them Kubistans. Exceptionally fine Kubas made in the 16th century are to be found in many museums, sometimes described as 'Armenian'. There are also many beautiful 19th-century examples. The ground is usually dark blue or red, the border ivory-white. Broad stripes decorated with leaves and flowers, and palmettes are the main design elements.

Kuduani. Dark coloured carpet produced by the Baluchi tribes. Unlike the 'Arab', also made by the Baluchis, which is ribbed on the back, the Kuduani is smooth and almost velvety.

Kufi. The angular Kufic script is found as a decorative element on the so-called Holbein carpets and on Caucasian carpets made at the end of the 18th and the beginning of the 19th centuries.

Kula. Turkish rugs. Closely resemble Ghiordes (q.v.). One kind, with a design consisting of groups of small cypresses, has been called the graveyard Kula.

Kumkapu. Suburb of Istanbul. Attractive Kumkapu rugs have been woven by Armenian girls since the beginning of the century, but few specimens exist today.

Kurdish Carpets. From Persian Kurdistan, usually made with woollen warp-threads and geometric in design.

Kure-Sumakh. See SUMAKH.

Kurk. Highly valued winter coat taken from the necks of sheep and goats and woven into precious fabrics—even more rarely into very finely hand-knotted small carpets and rugs.

Ladik. City of Asia Minor where, from the end of the 16th to well into the 19th century, very fine prayer-rugs were made. Distinguished in the design by three small prayer-alcoves, the arches of which are supported by slender columns. The ground is generally red.

Lahore Carpet. It was in Lahore, probably in the 16th and certainly by the 17th century, that the style of Indian carpet design, inasmuch as it differed from Persian, was first established. See also INDIAN CARPETS.

Lanceolate Leaves. Unidentified leaf shape resembling a

Lanceolate Leaves

287

spear-head often found in the design of Persian carpets. Especially associated with the Herati design.

Laver Kirman Rugs. See KIRMAN-LAVERS. The oldest type of Kirmans.

Lesghi. A Caucasian tribe which makes Lesghian rugs, in character scarcely distinguishable from Daghestans (q.v.).

'Lie' or 'Set' of Pile. It is not generally realised that there is an ideal position in which to lay a carpet in a room—nor is it always practical. This position is one in which either the light shines into the pile, or, if this is not possible, one's most frequent view of the carpet is looking into the pile. In this arrangement the colours emerge more richly.

Looped Pile Carpet. Carpet woven in loops, in the manner of velvet, which are afterwards cut.

Lours. Region in Central Persia between Ispahan and Kirmansha. The tribesmen make a thick rug, the ground colour of which is often deep indigo. A golden-yellow verging on orange is a distinctive colour used in the general theme.

Lozenge-shaped. A hooked motif commonly used in the Caucasian and Central Asian 'nomad carpets'. The 'lozenges' have hooks around them, those on the left side inclining to the right and vice versa on the right side.

'Meander Border.' A swastika-like pattern found in Chinese Turkestan carpets.

Medachyl. Persian name for the reciprocal crenellated motif.

Medallion Design. The medallion is a familiar decorative motif in Eastern art and much used as an element of design in Persian carpets.

Medjidieh-Ghiordes. Translated, means 'Mosque-carpet' or prayer-rug. The carpets given this name are more European than typically Oriental in style.

Mehrevan. Madder-red and dark blue are the predominant colours of this carpet, the design of which often consists of one or more medallions with corner pieces.

'Meander Border'

Medachyl motif

Medallion Design

Mekri. A district in south-east Smyrna where in the 18th and probably throughout the 19th century carpets resembling Bergamos were made, often with small floral designs and an ivory background.

Melas. Also spelled Meles and Melez. Anatolian prayer-rugs distinguished by a metallic, greenish yellow used in the colour scheme.

Merton Abbey Tapestry. Made at the Merton Abbey Tapestry works founded by William Morris in 1881.

Meshed Carpet. Meshed is the capital of Khorassan. The carpets so called are made of a soft and lustrous wool. The palm-leaf pattern is much used, as is the Herati design.

Met-Hané (Mechdi-Hané). The finest kind of Gendje rug (q.v.). A special feature of these rugs is their plain coloured ground.

Mianeh. City on the old route from Tabriz to Teheran, famous in particular for the production of Keleïs (q.v.), thick-piled, with floral patterns, and brightly coloured.

Mihrab motif

Mianeh-Keleï. Small Keleï (q.v.). Mianeh is Persian for 'a half'.

Mihrab. Prayer-niche or alcove in a mosque, represented in the design of Eastern carpets and prayer-rugs by a quadrilateral shape with a pointed arch at the top. When a Mohammedan prays he stands at the lower end of the rug and places some earth from Mecca in the spandrel of the Mihrab so that when he kneels he can touch the earth with his forehead.

Mina-Chané. Persian name for rosette-like pattern.

Ming Emblems. That of the phoenix fighting the dragon is occasionally to be found in Oriental carpets.

Mir-Sarabend Rugs. The finest of the old Sarabends (q.v.), incorporating the typical pear design.

Miri. Persian name for the palm-leaf motif (not to be confused with the palmette).

Mirzapore. Cheap quality Indian carpet. Many have been imported into Britain.

Mitres. Cross-joins on the back of a carpet. This method is in contrast with the carrying of the weft-threads directly from one side of the carpet to the other.

Mogan. The Mogan steppe extends from the shore of the Caspian Sea almost to Baku. In the second half of the 19th century fine carpets resembling Shirvans were made in this region.

Moorfields Carpets. Fine hand-knotted carpets were made by Thomas Moore of Moorfields from the mid-18th century. Robert Adam contributed a number of designs for these carpets, of which he made much use.

Moquette. Upholstery or carpet material woven with coarse wool and linen on the same principle as velvet.

Morocco. Coarsely knotted, dry carpets are made in Morocco, but they are not calculated to withstand hard wear.

Mina-Chané pattern   **Ming Emblem**

Morris, William. Made his first carpets at Hammersmith in 1878, later at Merton Abbey. The two- and three-ply carpets were woven for Morris & Co. in Yorkshire. See also MERTON ABBEY TAPESTRY.

Mortlake Tapestries. The Mortlake factory was active as early as 1620, working largely for the Court. Charles I, both as Prince of Wales and as King, took considerable interest in the enterprise, which also earned great esteem on the Continent.

Mosul Rugs. Have been described as the poorest of all Hamadan rugs; they have bright red fields and, as a rule, small angular medallions.

Mud. Trade name for the finest of Khorassan carpets; they have a close-cut pile and are often designed with a pattern of small palm-tree tops.

Mudjar. A very attractive Anatolian prayer-rug, usually containing a madder-red Mihrab. Less expensive than the Ghiordes, the Kulas, and the Ladiks.

Murdshakhar. Village between Sultanabad and Ispahan where finely knotted carpets are made with geometrical allover patterns.

Mushkebad Rugs. Resemble in design the Mahals, the Araks, and the Sultanabads—but are inferior in quality to all these three. The later examples have a red field and an allover design.

Nachl-I-Frangh. Persian term for 'European design', meaning rococo or Louis-Philippe.

Nadir Shah. After the conquest of Afghanistan in 1735 he sent the craftsmen of Herat, including the carpet-makers, to Persia where his people could learn their skills.

Nain Rugs. Nain Rugs and carpets have been described as the finest woven of their kind made in Iran since the war. Designs are derived from the old Ispahans, incorporating the Shah Abbas, Tulip and rosette motifs, with a light-coloured field.

Namasé. The word derives from *Djanemas*, meaning 'prayer-rug'.

Namaslyk. Colloquialism for NAMASÉ.

Needlework Carpets. In the 16th and 17th centuries it was a frequent custom in Europe to copy Oriental carpets in cross- and tent-stitch for table and cupboard coverings.

Nigde. In Asia Minor. Once the source of excellent quality prayer-rugs—now the centre of production of cheap, inferior-quality rugs.

Nil. Persian for indigo.

Niris Rugs. Frequently confused with Shiraz rugs. Favourite design—the large floriated pear.

Norway. Double cloth rugs for covers and cushions were made in Norway in the 18th and 19th centuries. The looped pile technique was seldom used.

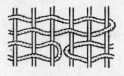

Palas weave   **Palmette design**

Norwich Carpets. Cloth carpeting and moquette are attributed to Norwich manufacture in the 17th century.

Oushak. Carpets have been made in this ancient Turkish city for 400 years. Oushaks may be seen in 15th- and 17th-century Dutch paintings. Later examples are coarse and inferior— bright turkey red with geometric designs in bright blues and green.

Pakistani Rugs. Many of these well made and moderately priced rugs are exported in Persian Tabriz and Royal Bokhara designs.

Palas. Known in Turkey as Kelims. These are not knotted, but flat-woven carpets, used in the East as floor-coverings over an underlay, as awnings for carts, wrappings for merchandise, etc.

Palm-leaves. See MIRI.

Palmette. Chief design component of the Herati border.

Pandermas. One of the leading Turkish rug exports since the beginning of this century. Brightly coloured, frequently with a cream ground, they are usually found in the traditional prayer-rug design.

Patterns. In the factory carpets are made to designs previously indicated in every detail; when making carpets for his own use the peasant works from his knowledge of the traditional elements of design, but improvises as to detail while he works at his loom.

Polygon ornament

Peking Rugs. Rugs hand-woven in Japan in antique Chinese designs, mainly in light beige, tan, green and gold.

Pendehs. See KISIL-AJAK.

Perdé. Translated, means 'curtain'. Employed as a dimensional term to indicate the next size larger than the Sedjadé (q.v.).

Persian. The Persian rug or carpet is usually oblong in shape, of a very fine and skilful weave, of a silk or wool pile, in traditional (frequently geometrical) patterns.

Peschm-I-Meshed. 'Wool from Meshed.' Name given to the very finest closely woven Heris (q.v.).

Petag. Abbreviation of Persische Teppich-Gesellschaft—the Persian Carpet Company in Tabriz. This company's productions have been described as the finest examples of the modern carpet-weaving industry in the Orient.

Petrovsk. Caucasian carpet-producing centre. Output is represented more by flat-woven than hand-knotted carpets.

Pictorial Carpets. Few, if any, of outstanding artistic merit would seem to have appeared since the splendid old hunting and animal carpets. See also HUNTING-CARPETS.

Pile. 'Face' of the carpet, i.e. the clipped surface.

Pillar Carpets. Carpets made for covering the pillars of a mosque or palace.

Pillar Ladiks. Trade name for a prayer-rug made in Asia Minor, having a design element common to certain Kulas and Melas carpets—the prayer-niche resting on two slender columns rising from a plinth.

Poland. In the 18th and 19th centuries many Kelim rugs, similar to those of Rumania and the Ukraine, were woven in Poland. Some knotted pile carpets in the European style and of excellent quality are known to have been made in the 17th century.

Polygon. Eight-, sixteen-, or multi-sided ornament common to Central Asiatic carpets.

Pomegranate design

Rosette motif

Pomegranate Design. Design found on antique Persian, and Chinese-Turkestan carpets from the 18th century.

Prayer-rugs. Oriental rugs having the 'Mihrab' design, based on the altar of the Mohammedan mosque, as the central feature.

Prophet or Prophet's Green. A darkish green with a tinge of orange, the colour sacred to Mahomet.

Pushti. Dimensional term applied to the very smallest Shiraz rugs.

Regh. 'The gauge'—the coarseness or fineness—of the stitch of a carpet.

Resht Patchwork. A mosaic patchwork applied to Persian covers and prayer-rugs in the 18th and 19th centuries, employing coloured felts and silks.

Ribbed Back. Where the warp-threads protrude on the back of a carpet in ribs or corrugations.

Rosette. Motif resembling flower-petals arranged in a circle in the manner of blades of a propeller.

Rumania. In the 18th and 19th centuries tapestry-woven rugs were produced in almost every village in Rumania, some with lozenge and geometric patterns, others with floral designs.

Runas. Persian word for madder.

Running Hound. Descriptive of a pattern of repeated triangular-shaped figures.

Ryijy Rugs. Finnish rugs made from the 17th century with rough, shaggy designs.

 **Running Hound pattern**

Saer. Persian linear measure (approx. 42¾ inches).

Safid-Feraghan. There are many Feraghans, the most famous of these being the Mahi. Some resemble European carpets of the 18th century. The prefix 'Safid' means white in Persian and denotes a light ground which stands out in relief against a darker border.

Saidabads. Fine, lustrous rugs of the Afshari groups, distinguished by an irregularity of weave detected on the ribbing on the back of the rug.

Salian. Small Caucasian city. Particularly beautiful, lustrous carpets of geometric pattern were produced in Salian in the present century.

Salor Rugs. Described as the finest of all Bokharas, with wine-coloured field and geometric borders.

Samarkand. Famous as a carpet bazaar. Numerous hand-woven carpets, such as those of Chotan, Kashgar, Yarkand, etc., are loosely referred to as Samarkands. The genuine antique Samarkands show a strong Chinese influence.

Saph. Anatolian family prayer-rug. Many early examples bore a pattern of paired shoe-prints.

Ryiji Rug design

Sarab. Region in the Bagshaish district where carpets are made similar to Yoraghan and Heris carpets.

Sarabend Rugs. Persian rugs characterised by a red or deep blue field and a motif consisting of rows of pears.

Sarajevo. Kelims, distinguished by their notably purple tone, were produced in this Jugoslav city up to the beginning of the present century.

Sarenim. Dimensional term; term also commonly applied to rugs from the Hamadan district.

Sarouk (or Saruk) Carpets. Woven in the city of Sultanabad—for the most part, heavy, tightly woven, with overall floral design.

Sarquart. Dimensional term.

Saryk Rugs (or Saryk Bokhara or Saryk Turkoman Rugs). Usually found with a shade of red field and three or more vertical rows of regular octagons.

Saveh. Carpet-making district to the north-west of the holy city of Kum.

Savonnerie Carpets. Originally made in France in the Oriental manner or in the manner of tapestry (Aubusson)—now made in India and Japan. Indian examples are soft-coloured, the Japanese Imperial Savonneries are heavy and durable.

Scotch Carpets. Also known as Kidderminster or Ingrain. Double-cloth or ply weavings.

Sedjadé. Dimensional term applied to Persian rugs of about 3 feet 4 inches to 4 feet 4 inches in width and 6 to 7 feet in length.

Sehna Knot. Knot used in Persian carpets from Sehna, Ispahan, Tabriz (also the Ghiordes knot), Saruk, Sarabend, Feraghan, Kerman, Shiraz and Herat.

Seichur. Village in the eastern Caucasus notable for the production of fine, lustrous wool rugs decorated with wide, richly ornamented medallions from which beam-like shapes emanate in diagonal directions.

Seljuk Carpets. Date from the 15th or even the 14th century. The oldest known complete carpets are the Seljuks in the Evkaf Museum at Istanbul.

 Sehna knot

Semnan Carpets. Fine-quality carpets similar to Teherans and Ispahans.

Sena Rugs (also spelled Senna and Senneh). The finest stitched of all Persian carpets. The patterns are either composed of small floral designs, or large richly decorated medallions reaching almost to the corners.

Sendshan Rugs. Cheap rugs decorated with the Persian flower and leaf ornaments in diminutive form.

Set. Trade term for carpets made in the same pattern or design, regardless of size.

Shaddas Rugs. Caucasian rugs, having loosely hanging threads on the back, with geometric patterns—mostly of small stylised leaves and flowers.

Shah Abbas. Celebrated ruler of Persia, during whose reign the country experienced an unprecedented renaissance in the art of carpet-weaving. What has come to be known as the Shah Abbas pattern is a design of different forms of palmette.

Sheldon Tapestry. William Sheldon, who set up his factory about the middle of the 16th century, was one of the earliest tapestry weavers in England whose work can be identified today.

Shellac. An Indian dye employed in Hamadan and Shiraz carpets dating from the middle of the 19th century.

Shiralby (or Shir-Ali-Bey). Caucasian carpet pattern consisting of geometrically formed palm-leaves.

Shiraz Rugs. See KASHKAIS.

Shah Abbas pattern

Shirvan Rug

Shiraz-Torki (or Turki). Nomadic tribe with a reputation as weavers, according to one authority, unsurpassed in Persia.

Shirazi. Term applied to the binding with wool of the warp-threads, two or three in number, on the longer sides of rugs and carpets.

Shirvan Rugs. In weave, thickness, and finish closely related to Kubas, Kabistans, Chi-chis, Bakus and Daghestans. In design, geometric.

Shirvan-Palas. Often used as door curtains, bale wrappings, etc., these palas are flat-woven. They are hard-wearing enough to act as floor-coverings.

Sil-I-Sultan (or Sil-e-Sultan). Term applied to carpets with a particular pattern—a motif of small stylised flowers (usually roses) endlessly repeated.

Siles. Caucasian flat-woven rugs, almost always made in two pieces which are afterwards sewn together.

Sivas. Finely woven Turkish rugs with a short-clipped nap.

Smyrna. 'Smyrna' or Turkey carpets having been made in various parts of Asia Minor since the 17th century. Until comparatively recently they could be distinguished from other Oriental carpets by their considerably greater depth of pile.

Soho Tapestry. From the end of the 17th century Soho became the main centre of English tapestry weaving. John Vanderbank, Paul Saunders and Joshua Morris were the leading weavers in the district during the 18th century.

Souchbulagh. Small city in northern Kurdistan where carpets of excellent quality and brilliant, attractive colouring have been made for centuries.

Soumak Rugs. Pileless Caucasian carpets with loose ends of stitch yarn at the back—invariably geometric in pattern.

Spain. Hispano-Moresque carpets were made in Spain in the early Middle Ages, and were generally woven with a single warp knot.

Sparta Rugs. Woven in Turkey and Greece, of relatively poor quality, often using Persian designs.

Streaks or Mottling. (Abrasch.) Blemishes in a yarn dyed with vegetable dye, comparable with flaws in genuine emeralds or rubies.

Sultanabad. The Sultanabad of Arak weaving area is one of the five largest in Iran. Here and hereabout thousands of Sarouks have been produced and exported. Sultanabad rugs, not finely woven but durable, are regarded as half-brothers of the more expensive Sarouks.

Sumakh. Flat-woven rug, very thick and warm to the feet—mostly red and blue in colour.

Surmey (or Suermey). The deepest tone of indigo.

Soumak Rug weave.   Spain: single warp knot.   Swastika device

Sutural or Seamed Border. Pattern composed of a series of adjacent triangles found in the narrow guards parallel to the borders of rugs.

Swastika. The Swastika, fylfot or crooked cross, is frequently used as a device on modern Persian carpets—also forms part of the 'meander border' used in Chinese Turkestan.

Sweden. Knotted-pile rugs, as in Finland (q.v.), were made in Sweden, in addition to double-cloth weavings, throughout the 18th and 19th centuries.

Syrian Carpets. Modern versions are coarse, and unattractive. Antique Syrian carpets known as 'Damascus carpets' are believed to have been produced in Egypt.

Tabachi. 'Tannery' wool, the wool of the fleece removed with lime from dead sheep.

Tabriz. Tabriz rugs of modern production are more stiffly formal in design than other Persian rugs. Tabriz is also the market place for Karaja, Ardebil, and Serab rugs.

Taibaff. The Muds and the Taibaffs are two especially fine carpets produced in Khorassan.

Talish. Caucasian rugs of glossy wool, dyed with indigo, madder and Isperek, with traditional geometric patterns.

Tcherkess Kazak Rugs. Thick, heavy rug bearing the 'Sunburst' or 'Russian coat of arms' design, sometimes known as 'The Palace Design'.

Teheran Rug. Notable for their extreme close cut, which often makes the design difficult to trace in detail.

Tekke Rugs or Tekke Bokhara Rugs. One of the finest woven of rugs with a short nap and geometric design with three rows of octagons.

Tekke Turkoman. See TEKKE RUGS.

Teramis. Village in Sultanabad where Sedjadés of fine quality wool are produced.

Terh-Mustuphi. Pattern of roses reproduced in naturalistic style.

Torbas. Turkoman name for pocket-like bags hung on the inside of tents as receptacles for all kinds of small objects.

Transylvania. Magnificent prayer-rugs were exported from Transylvania at the end of the 19th century.

Tribunal Carpets. See SET.

Turkey Carpet. Generic term to describe carpet made of wool with a thick pile and bold design mainly in red, blue and green.

Turkey Work. Term used in 16th- and 17th-century inventories to describe carpets, cushions and upholstery knotted in the fashion of Near Eastern rugs.

Turkibaff Rugs. Close-cut and brightly coloured—made in all sizes. The word 'turkibaff' or 'turkbaff' means 'Turkish knots'.

Turkish Rugs. Mostly from Anatolia and Asia Minor, imported from the 18th century onwards—originally used as wall hangings and table coverings.

Turkoman Rugs. Woven in traditional variations of the same motif—octagonal gules, known as 'elephant's foot' and generally dyed in a deep Turanian red.

Turshis or Turchus. The most coarsely woven of the Khorassan carpets (q.v.).

Ukraine. Tapestry woven rugs were a flourishing peasant craft in the Ukraine. Some of these rugs bear the Turkish influence, others the Bessarabian motif—a sprawling floral pattern. By the middle of the 19th century Western Europe provided the model for many designs.

Vase Carpets. Principally made in Tabriz. Some contain a

Turkoman Rug gules motif

pattern of one or more vases with a tracery of shoots and palmettes. Sometimes the latter features alone are present, the vases absent.

Veramin. A town to the south-east of Teheran. Veramin rugs and carpets are particularly beautiful and lustrous, sometimes very dark in colour, having as their ruling pattern small flowers and leaves.

Vernés. Caucasian carpets, similar to the Sumakhs, with a distinctive pattern consisting of a small square within a large one, with other small squares surrounding it containing lozenge-shaped figures.

Wavy Shoots or Wavy Tendrils. Continuous motif found in the narrow guards of borders.

Wilton Carpets. Wool or worsted carpets with a very short, thick pile, resembling Brussels carpets, first made at Wilton.

Yapraks. Anatolian carpets made in the 19th century with a design of stylised leaves—a variant of palmettes.

Yarkand. City in Chinese Turkestan. The carpets produced in Yarkand are strongly Chinese in influence, with Chinese floral ornamentation and symbols.

Yastiks. The Turkish name for small bedside mats.

Yesd Carpets. Similar to the older Kirmans, with a design of medallions and flowers.

Yomud Rugs. Very fine carpets with a brownish-red ground, often with a tinge of violet, and a polygon or lozenge-shaped figure motif.

Yoraghan. Coarse to medium-fine carpet woven in the Bagshaish district—the design in most cases being a medallion with corners.

Yuruks. Shaggy Anatolian rugs frequently sold by dealers as Sultans.

Ziegler. Ziegler and Co., a Manchester firm, established a strong foothold in Persia in the 1860s. 'Ziegler carpets', made in Sultanabad, are of soft, pastel colours, using the most excellent wool.

PART SEVEN

Some Craftsmen and Manufacturers

Absolon, William (1751–1815). Pottery decorator and china and glass dealer at Yarmouth. His mark, 'Absolon Yarme No 25', painted in red, accompanies the makers' marks on certain wares of Turner, Wedgwood, Shorthose and Leeds.

Adam, Robert (1728–92). Eminent architect and designer of furniture.

Affleck, Thomas. American cabinet-maker, who was born in Aberdeen and went with John Penn to Philadelphia in 1736 as resident cabinet-maker. He died there in 1795.

Alcock (S) & Co. Burslem pottery firm noted for its manufacture of moulded figures in relief.

Allen, Robert. Enameller of white porcelain working at Lowestoft, Suffolk, from the mid-18th century.

Allgood Family. Edward, John and William. Made japanned goods at Pontypool from 1730–1818, and at Usk from 1761.

Allison, Michael. Early 19th-century cabinet-maker of New York. His work is sometimes confused with that of Duncan Phyfe.

Appleton, Nathaniel. Early 19th-century cabinet-maker from Salem, Mass., who specialised in federal-style furniture.

Ash, Gilbert. New York cabinet-maker (1717–85), who made some of the earliest American Chippendale-style furniture.

Bacon, John (1740–99). Sculptor and porcelain modeller.

Banford, James (1724–87). A Battersea enameller.

Barker, Benjamin. An artist from Bath who was employed by William Allgood as foreman decorator at the Pontypool Japan Works in the late 18th century, specialising in sporting scenes.

Bateman, Hester. Registered her goldsmith's mark 1774–6. Her firm was responsible for a range of neo-classical ware.

Baxter, Thomas. 18th-century china painter who worked, for the most part, at the Worcester factory.

Beckett Family. Benjamin, Edward, Isaac and Susannah. Enamellers at Bilston in the 18th century.

Beneman, Jean Guillaume. A German who became known as a cabinet-maker in Paris in the late 18th century and made furniture for the Court.

Bennett (Edwin) Pottery Co. Bennett was an English potter who established himself in Baltimore, U.S.A., in the mid-19th century. The factory produced Rockingham and yellow ware, but was probably best known for the so-called 'Rebekah' teapots.

Berain, Jean (1638–1711). Belgian draughtsman and designer, who designed for Boulle. Work in his style is described as Berainesque.

Bickley, Benjamin. Enameller at Bilston in the 18th century.

Billingsley, William (1760–1828). China painter and arcanist, associated at one time or another with the Derby, Pinxton, Mansfield and Torksey factories.

Boote, T. & R. Succeeded to the Waterloo Pottery at Burslem in the mid-19th century; makers of Parian ware, encaustic tiles and earthenware.

Bottengruber, Ignaz. 18th-century German porcelain decorator, examples of whose work can be found on Meissen and Vienna porcelain.

Boulton, Matthew (1728–1809). Fine metalwork manufacturer; credited with the production of some of the outstanding enamels made at the Birmingham factory of Boulton and Fothergill.

Bourne & Sons. Early 19th-century stoneware manufacturers. The business is still in existence.

Briand, Thomas. An 18th-century chemist who experimented in soft-paste porcelain and was one of the founders of the Chelsea porcelain factory.

Brooks, John. 18th-century Dublin engraver, one-time partner of Janssen and Delamain at Battersea. Probably the initiator of transfer printing on enamel and china.

Burling, Thomas. New York cabinet-maker, who died in 1800, whose label is still occasionally found. He made a writing desk for George Washington's first official residence as President.

Carré, Jean. 16th-century Belgian glass-maker who set up in business in London, making glasses in the Venetian manner.

Chaffers, William. Editor of *Marks and Monograms on Pottery and Porcelain*, published in 1863. He has been held responsible for incorrectly ascribing a large quantity of Chinese porcelain to the Lowestoft factory in England.

Chamberlain, Robert. Porcelain painter who, in 1783, left the old company of Worcester porcelain makers and started up on his own. Eventually, in 1862, the new company became known as the Royal Worcester Porcelain Company.

Champion, Richard (1743–91). Porcelain manufacturer, of Bristol.

Chapin, Elephet (1741–1807). One of a Connecticut family of furniture makers, who used cherrywood for their Chippendale style highboys and secretaires, instead of the more usual mahogany.

Chippendale, Thomas (1718–79). A London cabinet-maker, whose designs in *The Gentleman and Cabinet-makers' Director* (1754) were widely adopted. Chippendale furniture therefore does not necessarily mean pieces made in his workshop, but merely according to his designs.

Coffee, William. 18th-century porcelain modeller and maker of terracotta.

Cogswell, John. Boston cabinet-maker, well known in the

latter half of the 18th century for his Chippendale bookcases and chests of drawers.

Cookworthy, William (1705–80). Successful experimenter in hard paste. The patent was acquired by Richard Champion (q.v.).

Copland, H. Collaborator with Matthias Lock in books on furniture design in the mid-18th century. It is probable that they were the producers of many of the plates in Chippendale's *Director*.

Cressent, Charles. French cabinet-maker who started his career as a sculptor and was well known in Paris in the first half of the 18th century.

Daniel, Ralph. Staffordshire potter, supposed to have been the first English enameller of salt-glazed stoneware; also credited with the introduction before 1750 of plaster-of-Paris moulds.

Davenport Family. Proprietors of Brindley's Pottery from 1793. Until early in the 19th century production was confined to earthenware; later, china was produced in the Derby style.

Delamain, Henry. Partner with Janssen in the 18th-century Battersea enamel venture.

Disbowe, Nicholas. The first known American furniture maker, who was born in Walden, Essex, where his father was a joiner, and who settled in Hartford, Connecticut, before 1639.

Dunlop, Samuel, II (1751–1830). New Hampshire cabinet-maker, specialising in maple tallboys and secretaires.

Edgerton, Matthew. Well known New Brunswick cabinet-maker in the late 18th century. Some fine examples of his work are still in existence.

Elfe, Thomas. Prominent cabinet-maker in Charleston, S. Carolina, in the second half of the 18th century, in the Chippendale style.

Elliot, John. Philadelphia cabinet-maker in the second half of the 18th century, specialising in wall mirrors.

Fabergé, Peter Carl (1846–1920). The celebrated Russian jeweller. The articles made under his supervision by the five hundred or so skilled workmen he employed display the finest craftsmanship of the time. Particular fame attached to the magnificent Easter Eggs, each containing a new surprise, which he designed and presented annually to the Czar of Russia as a gift for the Czarina.

Flitcroft, Henry (1697–1769). A joiner who became an architect and was one of the Palladian builders who also designed furniture.

Folwell, John. Late 18th-century cabinet-maker of Philadelphia, sometimes called 'the Chippendale of America'.

Frothingham, Benjamin. Late 18th-century cabinet-maker of Charlestown, Mass. Some of his work still to be found bearing his label.

Games, James. Early 18th-century cabinet-maker of Ipswich, Mass., possibly the originator of certain developments on Queen Anne chairs.

Gaudreau, Antoine Robert. French cabinet-maker who worked for the crown from 1726.

Gibbons, Grinling (1648–1721). Carver and designer, born at Rotterdam. He was discovered by John Evelyn in Deptford in 1671, and was used by Wren to do carving in St Pauls and other London churches. He also carved ornate picture frames and other decorations for several country houses.

Giles, James (1718–80). Enameller of Bow, Worcester, and other porcelains.

Gillingham, James. Philadelphia cabinet-maker of the mid-18th century, noted for 'Gothic' Chippendale chairs.

Gillow Family. Robert Gillow, founder of the furniture-making firm, was an 18th-century joiner in Lancaster, whose furniture was sent to London and other places. Business carried on by his descendants.

Gimson, Ernest (1864–1919). A disciple of William Morris whom he met in 1884 and who did much to encourage a revival of furniture craftsmanship.

Goddard, James. Well-known Rhode Island furniture-maker of the mid-18th century, noted for block front and shell carved work.

Goodison, Benjamin. 18th-century London cabinet-maker with workshop in Long Acre.

Gostelowe, Jonathan. Philadelphia cabinet-maker of the late 18th century, noted for original work of his own design.

Grendey, Giles (1693–1780). A joiner and chair-maker who became Master of the Worshipful Company of Joiners in 1766.

Gumley, John. Early 18th-century looking-glass maker at Lambeth and later cabinet-maker to George I. Died 1729.

Haig, Thomas. 18th-century cabinet-maker who was in partnership with Thomas Chippendale and later with his son, Thomas Chippendale, the younger.

Halfpenny, William and John. A father and son who were chiefly known as architects and published *Rural Architecture in the Chinese Taste* (1757) and *New Designs for Chinese Temples* (1750). Their garden architecture also included designs for chairs and other furniture.

Hepplewhite, George. Famous 18th-century cabinet-maker who, like his contemporaries, Chippendale and Sheraton, gave his name to a whole school of furniture based on the designs in his book *The Cabinet Makers' and Upholsterers' Guide*. He was apprenticed to the firm of Gillow. Died 1786.

Hope, Thomas (1769–1831). A Regency connoisseur who published *Household Furniture and Interior Decoration*, 1807, a book of designs which were used for furnishing his own house.

Hosner, Joseph. Late 18th-century cabinet-maker of Concord, Mass., who worked chiefly in cherry and other New England woods.

Ince and Mayhew. Famous 18th-century cabinet-makers. Authors of the *Universal System of Household Furniture*.

Jacob, George. 18th-century French cabinet-maker, who specialised in chairs. His mark is also to be found on a number of beds of the period.

Janssen, Stephen Theodore. Merchant stationer and patron of the arts, who started the painted enamel venture at York House, Battersea, in 1753. Was Lord Mayor of London, 1754.

Jensen, Gerreit. Late 17th- and early 18th-century cabinet-maker who supplied the Royal Household in the reign of William and Mary.

Johnson, Thomas. 18th-century designer and wood-carver, who worked in Soho. Author of *One Hundred and Fifty New Designs* (1761).

Kent, William (1686–1748). One of the first architects to pay much attention to the interior and furnishings of his houses, in which practice he was notably followed by Adam. Exponent of the Palladian style. His patron was the Earl of Burlington.

Lalique, René (1860–1945). French creator of elegantly designed and moulded objects, made by blowing and pressing, afterwards given a matt surface by acid or wheel engraving.

Lamerie, Paul de (1688–1751). Huguenot goldsmith who worked in London and who popularised the French Rococo manner in English silver.

Leleu, Jean François. French cabinet-maker, born in Paris in 1729.

Lemon, William. Master cabinet-maker of Salem, Mass., famous for his work in the Hepplewhite manner.

Linnell, John. 18th-century carver and cabinet-maker, who worked mainly to Chippendale designs. Died 1796.

Lock, Mathias (Fl. c. 1740–69). Designer. With W. H. Copland probably produced many of the plates for Chippendale's *Director*.

McIntyre, Samuel. Famous Salem architect, woodwork designer and carver (1757–1811).

Manwaring, Robert. Designer and cabinet-maker. Publisher of *The Cabinet and Chair-Makers' Real Friend and Companion* (1765) and *The Chair-makers' Guide* (1766).

Marot, Daniel (1663–1752). A French Huguenot architect, decorator and furniture designer, who worked for William III and became his Minister of Works. His designs reflected French taste.

Marsh and Tatham. Cabinet-makers who worked closely with Henry Holland and were much employed by the Prince Regent.

Moore, Robert. One of three brothers, all prominent 18th-century Baltimore cabinet-makers.

Neuber, Johann Christian (1736–1808). Celebrated as maker of exquisite snuff-boxes in hard stones.

Neville, George. Made a fortune from the introduction in the 1830s of painting on papier-mâché.

Oeben, Jean Francois. Famous French cabinet-maker born c. 1720, who worked for Boulle and the Gobelins firm, and was at one time *Ébéniste du Roi*.

Palmer, Humphrey. 18th-century potter of Hanley (Staffs) and rival of Wedgwood in the manufacture of black basaltes and jasperware.

Pardoe, Thomas (1770–1823). Painter and independent enameller. Examples of his work are found on Derby, Worcester, Swansea, Nantgarw and Coalport porcelain.

Perry, Edward. Manufacturer of papier-mâché, who started his career in Wolverhampton in the early 19th century.

Phyfe, Duncan. Master cabinet-maker, who emigrated from Scotland to New York, where he made a great reputation producing furniture in the Sheraton and Directoire style. Died in 1854.

Preissler, Daniel (1636–1733). Believed to have been the first person to apply black monochrome decoration, known as Schwarzlot, to porcelain.

Randolph, Benjamin. 18th-century American cabinet-maker;

leading exponent of the Chippendale school. Worked in Philadelphia.

Raven, Samuel. 19th-century Birmingham decorator of japanned snuff-box lids, cigar cases, etc.

Ravenet, Simon-François (1706–74). French engraver who worked on the perfection of the transfer printing method at the Battersea enamel factory from c. 1750.

Ravenscroft, George (1618–81). Glassmaker and experimenter. Associated with the introduction of flint glass or glass of lead, which gave English glass an advantage over foreign imports. The first glassmaker to mark his work with a seal—a raven's head.

Rittenhouse, David (1732–96). Astronomer, inventor and clock-maker of Philadelphia.

Rose, John. Founder of the Coalport factory, Shropshire, in 1795, absorbing the Caughley firm, to which he had been apprenticed.

Sadler, John and Guy Green. 18th-century transfer-printers for Wedgwood and other firms.

Sanderson, Elijah (1751–1825). Salem cabinet-maker.

Savery, William (1721–87). Notable Philadelphian cabinet-maker. Made a wide range of furniture from rush-bottom chairs to Chippendale tallboys.

Schaper, Johann (1621–70). Pottery and glass painter, mostly in black. See also PREISSLER.

Seymour, John. Master cabinet-maker of Boston; particularly famous for his fine satinwood inlay work.

Shaw, John. Maryland cabinet-maker of the 18th century, who worked in the Hepplewhite and Sheraton tradition.

Shearer, George. Cabinet-maker and designer of the time of Hepplewhite and Sheraton.

Sheraton, Thomas (1751–1806). Famous designer of furniture. Publisher of *The Cabinet-Maker and Upholsterer's Drawing Book.*

Sherratt, Obadiah and Martha. 19th-century pottery figure and toy makers.

Spangler, Jean Jaques. 18th-century ceramic modeller.

Stalker and Parker. Authors of a 17th-century treatise on japanning.

Steele, Thomas (1772–1850). Porcelain decorator.

Storr, Paul. London goldsmith, working 1797 to 1821, to whom is attributed the creation of the Regency style in silver.

Taylor, John. Birmingham enameller who owned a large button factory and produced many small enamel buttons and snuff-boxes before the middle of the 18th century.

Tuft, Thomas. 18th-century cabinet-maker of the Philadelphia Chippendale school.

Vaucanson, Jaques de (1708–82). One of the earliest makers of automata.

Verzelini, Giacomo (1522–1606). Glassmaker to Queen Elizabeth. Manager of Jean Carré's glasshouse at Crutched Friars and later owner of a glasshouse in Broad Street.

Voyer, John (1735–1800). Immigrant French pottery modeller and manufacturer.

Wall, John (1708–76). Original shareholder in the Worcester porcelain factory; the reference 'Dr Wall period' is to the first period of Worcester porcelain.

Weaver, Holmes (1769–1848). Newport (Rhode Island) cabinet-maker, who worked in the Hepplewhite and Sheraton styles.

Webber, Henry. One of Josiah Wedgwood's modellers, who was employed on copying the Portland Vase (See Part One).

Wedgwood, Josiah (1730–95). The founder of the famous Wedgwood pottery works at Burslem who worked first as a 'thrower' and 'modeller', went into partnership with Thomas Whieldon to enlarge his experience, and built a model village for his workmen at his new works at Etruria.

Whieldon, Thomas. 18th-century Staffordshire potter known for wide range of ware—'agate', 'marbled', 'tortoiseshell', 'Astbury' and 'Jackfield'; also dappled earthenware and unglazed red stoneware, sometimes with 'scratch blue' patterns.

Wood, Ephraim. Enameller, and manufacturer of pottery figures, late 18th to early 19th century.

Yardley, Samuel. First recorded enameller in Wednesbury, Staffordshire; products noted for their distinctively white base, which carried brightly glossy decoration.

Bibliography

The Concise Encyclopaedia of Antiques, 5 vols. Edited by
L. G. G. Ramsey. Published by the *Connoisseur*.
An Encyclopaedia of Antiques, by Harold Lewis Bond. Tudor
Publishing Co.
The Plain Man's Guide to Antique Collecting, by Ernest Rey-
nolds. Michael Joseph.
Collecting Antiques, by G. Bernard Hughes. Country Life.
The Connoisseur's Handbook of Antique Collecting. Edited by
Helena Hayward. Published by the *Connoisseur*.
The Country Life Collector's Pocket Book, by G. Bernard
Hughes. Country Life.
The Country Life Pocket Book of China, by G. Bernard Hughes.
Country Life.
The Country Life Book of English China, by Geoffrey Wills.
Country Life.
The Collector's Dictionary of Glass, by E. M. Elville. Country
Life.
English, Scottish and Irish Table Glass, by G. Bernard Hughes.
Batsford.
English and Irish Cut Glass, by E. M. Elville. Country Life.
English Glass for the Collector: 1660–1860, by G. Bernard
Hughes. Lutterworth Press.
The Country Life Pocket Book of Glass, by Geoffrey Wills.
Country Life.
The Country Life Book of Glass, by Frank Davis. Country Life.
Small Antique Silverware, by G. Bernard Hughes. Batsford.
The Shorter Dictionary of English Furniture, by Ralph Edwards.
Country Life.

BIBLIOGRAPHY

English Furniture, by John C. Rogers. Country Life.

English Furniture Styles: 1500–1830, by Ralph Fastnedge. Penguin Books.

Decorative Furniture (English and French) of the 16th, 17th and 18th Centuries, by W. H. Hackett. London: Estates Gazette, Ltd.

The Plain Man's Guide to Second-Hand Furniture, by Frank Davis. Michael Joseph.

The Country Life Book of English Furniture, by Edward T. Joy. Country Life.

The Collector's Dictionary of Clocks, by H. Alan Lloyd. Country Life.

Oriental Rugs: a Complete Guide, by Charles W. Jacobsen. Prentice-Hall.

How to Know Oriental Carpets and Rugs, by Heinrich Jacoby. Allen & Unwin.